CH00544973

Movies

And

Me

A Fistful of Filmic Reflections

Special thanks to Martin for all your help
on this and lots of my other books.

Index

Page   Chapter

Early Showings.

I have some great memories of watching war movies and westerns with my dad. We probably watched them as a family but I particularly recall watching and discussing them with dad. He introduced me to films like *The Wooden Horse, I Was Monty's Double, Tobruk, The Caine Mutiny, High Noon, The Magnificent Seven, The Great Escape, The War Wagon, Ice Cold in Alex* and *Colditz*. Later we fell about to Peter Sellers in his Inspector Clouseau guise, and laughed uproariously to a little known comedy spaghetti western called *They Call Me Trinity*. I think I went along to those Saturday kids' matinees. Though the memories are hazy. Strange to think now that we used to sit in a rather smoky version of the dark – I think there were smoking and non-smoking sections back then.

Perching in the dark before a huge screen has always held a certain kind of thrill, though perhaps a little unnerving too. I went to see Disney's *Robin Hood* with our next-door neighbour and his dad, but when my mate's dad decided to take off for a while I found it hard to enjoy the film, as I got it into my head someone might sidle over and beat us up in the dark. The outside world has always seemed a mixed bag to me – full of opportunities muddled with the possibility of trouble. I cite *Whistle Down the Wind* as my first real cinema experience, a movie I still love to this day. I found it funny and gripping and of course fell for Hayley Mills immediately. These days I see so much more in it, so many parallels with aspects of the Christian faith. If you've not seen it, it's about three children who find a criminal in their family barn and mistake him for Jesus.

Two other early cinema trips stick in my mind, one to see a re-run of *The Longest Day*, how we loved that, and then to see my first James Bond *Diamonds are Forever*. This second film left me with the misconception that I would never understand a James Bond plot. I have since learned that it just happens to be a story that makes no sense. And bears no resemblance whatsoever to the Fleming original. It was only decades later when I read *On Her Majesty's Secret Service* that I discovered, joy of joys, I could actually make sense of what was going on! Eureka!

Along the way there were swashbucklers like Richard Lester's *Three Musketeers* and *Four Musketeers*, harassed heroes winning through in *Zulu, Beau Geste* and *Where Eagles Dare,* and the histrionic, daft, and wonderfully creepy *Carry on Screaming.* I probably saw most of the *Carry Ons* in my time, *Carry on Spying* comes to mind featuring codenamed heroes like Bluebottle, Red Admiral and Yellow Peril. And I used to watch quite a few of the Hammer Horror films, but haven't kept my passion for scary screeners. The only horror flick on my list of favourites is the fairly recent *Us*. I'm grateful for a vivid imagination but movie things that go bump and boo in the night tend to follow me home and keep me awake in the wee small hours. I lie there waiting for those bumps and boos to leap out and scare the Scooby Doo out of me.

At some point I went to see *101 Dalmatians*. Lots of cute puppies and the toppest of top villains Cruella Deville. It's one of the few Disney animations for which I still have a soft spot. No pun intended! I don't think I went along to see many Disney adventures on the big screen, but we did faithfully watch *Disney Time* on TV every bank holiday Monday. That featured short extracts from the Mouse studio's back catalogue. At one point I was given a small plastic hand cranked projector as a Christmas present. That came complete with four Disney shorts. I used to crouch in a darkened space between our bedrooms, the doors shut and lights off, watching these mini movies on the wall. I had no idea that those early cinematic forays would lead to this. I work as a real projectionist now, one evening a week. And thankfully the machine is not hand cranked.

Decades after seeing all those cute chaotic Dalmatians we watched the feline classic *The Aristocats* with our daughter. Now that's a fun watch. Especially the scenes with the coolest of cool cats Thomas O'Malley. I love his parting shot as he waves goodbye to Duchess, 'Aloha, auf wiedersehen, bonsoir, sayonara, and all those goodbye things, baby.'

Empire of the Sun.

For a long time after I first saw this Spielberg epic I named it as my favourite movie. I've seen so many films now that I find it hard to call a favourite, but it's still in my top five all these years later. It swept me up with great scene after great scene. The characters, the dialogue, the colours, the cinematography – though I doubt I would have called it that back in 1988. There was just something powerful and captivating about this heady mixture. I was a Spielberg fan anyway, and this story of a resourceful young boy in China, caught up in the horrors of war yet making the best of it, snuck into my head and stayed there. I didn't know who Christian Bale was back then, but his character Jim grabbed me by the lapels and hoicked me into his wondrous and brutal world. *Batman* Bale hasn't done too badly for himself since. These days he features in a clutch of my favourite films. I may not have known him then, but I did recognise John Malkovich, from *The Killing Fields*, and Nigel Havers, from *Chariots of Fire*. Two other films that mean a lot to me.

In 2002 it was *Empire of the Sun* that drew my eye to a book which would change my life. *Praying the Movies* featured a still of Christian Bale as young Jim on its cover, and I was soon owning a copy and reading bits of it on a daily basis. The author, Edward McNulty, was doing something I'd not come across before, he was taking mainstream films and using them as vehicles for reflecting on life and faith. Could it be possible to do this? Take something I really loved and use it as a means of connecting with

God? Were you *allowed* to do this? Use something so enjoyable for something so important? Really? In the few years leading up to this discovery I had been working in a multiplex. My wife and I had fallen on hard times and couldn't work out where to head next, so I ended up doing three part time jobs. One of which involved sweeping up popcorn, selling pick'n'mix and slipping in to watch twenty-minute chunks of the latest big screen movies. At the time I felt as if I was lost in a directionless wilderness, but it turned out I was actually in training for something a few years down the line.

By the time I came across Edward McNulty's book we had found a way forward and had joined the Lee Abbey Community in North Devon. A Christian holiday and retreat centre set in hundreds of acres of forest, farmland and countryside. Digital cameras were becoming all the rage and we had been given one as a Christmas present just before leaving to join this community. This meant that I had begun taking photos of various splashes of nature scattered around the estate. And having discovered the wonders of PowerPoint I began creating visual presentations of text and images for worship in the Lee Abbey conferences. This new multimedia approach, mixed with my love of film, and those experiences at the cinema all melded one day when a good friend Tim suggested I start showing bits of film in small group workshops to spark thought about faith and life. Boom!

I armed myself with a VCR and various videos, and set about showing short clips to illustrate biblical stories and themes, doing my best to start and stop the *magic lantern* at just the right moments to avoid assaulting the ears of the listeners with anything inappropriate. From the outset I was intent on using not just happy family-friendly clips, but other gritty, dramatic and difficult moments to highlight the humanity and struggles of those in the Bible. As I was struggling myself it was these things that were helping me at the time.

One of the moments I chose from *Empire of the Sun* involved Jim bowing down and offering his own back to be beaten by an incensed guard, in place of the doctor in the camp. (Played by the aforementioned Nigel Havers.) It seemed to me to say something about the offering and sacrifice of Jesus for our troubles. Stepping into our shoes, holding nothing back as he moves into our difficult neighbourhoods.

Ever since I was a boy I've had an interest in that war in the Far East, because my uncle (and godfather) had been captured by the Japanese and taken to work on what became known as The Death Railway. Prisoners of war were set to work on a supply line snaking from Siam (now Thailand) to Burma. The conditions were barbaric and it is said that one soldier died for every sleeper laid. My godfather drove trucks in that environment, and I only ever heard him talk of it on one occasion. And even then he paused for a moment before doing so.

As a teenager I had read *Miracle on the River Kwai*, about Ernest Gordon's experience on that railway, and how other Christians in the camp led him to an encounter with Jesus. However, when I sat down late one night to watch a film called *To End All Wars*, I had no idea what it was and switched it off. I only discovered years later that it was a film based on Ernest Gordon's book, and I promptly bought the DVD. I'm amazed now that I didn't watch it that first time, if only because it was about a subject that had always meant so much. The sacrifice of one of the Christians, a guy called Dusty, in both the book and the film is shocking and profoundly moving. It's a scene I have used from time to time.

My godfather was a Christian and remained one all his life. Even through those terrible years. He prayed for my dad and the rest of his family each evening in the prison camp. I believe he told my father about this the day dad and I got baptised. I recently came across a record of my uncle listed as a POW, on the website FEPOW (Far East Prisoners of War). It was a moving and profound moment to find myself reading his name and a few details on the official record of his time as a prisoner of war in Thailand.

Another favourite in our house was *The Bridge on the River Kwai*, another film about prisoners of war on the Burma-Siam railway. Yet I feel a little differently about it now. It's a great film, and we used to love watching it, the explosion of the bridge at the end was at that time the most expensive ever filmed by Hollywood. But now I have learned more about the real story. The film is based on a novelised version of events combined with a film treatment written for the producer Sam Spiegel. All movies change true stories in order to fit them into a cinematic format, but this film contains a fair number of inaccuracies and the portrayal of the senior officer is incorrect. In the film the character is Colonel Nicholson, in real life his name was Philip Toosey. Toosey did not transform into an officer intent on building the best bridge possible, the Japanese did all the engineering work, but rather he continued to do everything he could to support his suffering men. He was a servant-hearted and dedicated man. These days I'd suggest that *The Railway Man*, *To End All Wars*, or *Unbroken* present a more realistic take on the life of those POWs. You can find the true story about *The Bridge on the River Kwai* on YouTube, if you look up – 'Philip Toosey and the bridge on the river Kwai'. Toosey's granddaughter, historian Julie Summers, tells the real story.

Another early clip I used came from the death row movie *Green Mile* in which Tom Hanks befriends a giant of a guy headed for the chair. John Coffey displays an extraordinary gift for healing others. And on one occasion Hanks takes him out of prison to visit the dying wife of another of the guards. Although the woman is at first terrified and swears at Coffey, the big guy is undeterred; he sits quietly beside her and then removes the sickness from her body. This scene instantly made me think of the time when Jesus raised Jairus's daughter, and to a lesser degree, Elisha raising a boy in the Old Testament, in 2 Kings chapter 4. The scene in the film is charged with uncertainty and fear. Coffey is an unlikely hero here. As he sets to work healing the woman the house shakes a little.

Everything about this scene opened my eyes a little more and made me wonder about the ministry of Jesus. I doubt if houses shook when he was helping people, but who knows? Certainly the ground shook when he died, and again when he rose from the dead. And graves burst open too. So the physical world resonated with the power of God at work. Oddly, it was the woman swearing in this scene which really set me thinking. It struck me that Jesus would not have been phased one bit by the words which would make this scene unpleasant to some Christians. Especially when you consider the flak that Jesus lived with on a daily basis. He didn't operate in a hermetically sealed PG version of life. He saw and heard it all. Not just that which Paul describes as noble, pure, lovely, admirable, excellent and worthy of praise. (Although I get the point that he's making here in Philippians 4.) Jesus was never afraid of the seedy and wild side of life. He was totally earthed. Sleaze and grime never put him off. He came looking for those trapped in dark corners. Sometimes a moment from a film can help you see that in a new light.

Dead Poets Society.

Quite often it takes time for a film to grow on me. I saw this Robin Williams tale when it came out at the back end of 1989. I had just moved to High Wycombe and went with my friends and housemates, Chris and Soobie. At the time I thought it was interesting and okay. It was only years later, when life was collapsing around us, that I revisited the film on video and really began to appreciate it. To misquote Robin Williams's character Mr Keating – I started to suck the marrow from it. Since then I have used it many times, using the example of Mr Keating the poetry teacher to illustrate Jesus's engaging style of maverick and interactive teaching.

When I rediscovered the film it was one of the boys in the story, Todd, who really moved me. He was lacking in confidence and struggling to write his own poem. So much so that when he was asked to read his piece out in class, he had to confess he hadn't come up with anything. Mr Keating then tells the class that Todd feels that everything inside of him is worthless. Boy, did I get that. It moved me to tears. I knew that feeling of inadequacy and failure, that sense of confusion and loss of courage and direction. I had been working full time using drama and mime to communicate the Christian faith, and gradually, over a couple of years, the stress had increased, and I had lost my way. Having given it up in the hope that a writing career might take off I seemed to be going nowhere. And so I love the scene when Mr Keating refuses to give up on Todd and instead stands him in front of the class and coaxes a powerful piece of creativity from him. *Truth is like a blanket that always leaves your feet cold.* So says Todd as Mr Keating circles him, urging him on. How true that statement can be. Truth without love can be harsh and brittle, repelling us rather than drawing us closer. That's why I believe in the power of a good story to woo us, to create conversation and questions, to open us to the truth that sets us free. Rather than leaving us with chilly toes and frozen feet.

Jesus was a past master at drawing people out. He was never heavy handed with those who were lacking in confidence or faith. Never bludgeoned or coerced them. Like Mr Keating with Todd, he knew how to draw them out, and refused to give up on them. Peter would happily, or rather, unhappily, have gone back to fishing, restating his first response to Jesus. 'Go away from me Lord, I'm a sinful person. I say the wrong thing, and when I'm not putting my feet in my mouth, I'm tripping over them. And when the crunch came, I let you down. I ran from you, the words of denial screaming in my ears. I'm hopeless when it comes to being a disciple. Leave me alone.'

But Jesus wouldn't leave him alone. He knew there was more to him. Peter might feel as if everything inside of him was worthless but Jesus knew different. He knows that same truth about us all. About you and me. But he won't batter us with it, he'll draw us with kindness and compassion. Mercy and truth have kissed, the writer of Psalm 85 assures us. Well they certainly have in Jesus, and that's what he offers to us. The embrace of justice, peace, assurance and love.

Evan and Bruce Almighty.

Whilst working in the cinema I had a kind of epiphany moment. It happened while I was watching the Nicholas Cage film *Gone in 60 Seconds,* where a gang of well-meaning crooks steal a whole bunch of cars in a single night, to appease an ill-meaning crook who has threatened to kill one of them. I was thoroughly enjoying this caper when I had a thought – was I allowed to enjoy it? What did the critics think? Was this a good movie or not? I panicked. Just a little. And then I thought... who cares? A film is a film. If you enjoy it, enjoy it. I have, over the years, before and since that moment, done my best to adore or detest films that the critics like or detest. I've tried to do as I was told. But it's no good. I can't do it. And while I'm on the subject of critical acclaim, let me just throw in this solid gold nugget (or lump of coal depending on your viewpoint). No film should be hailed as 'an important film'. As if somehow the world might end if we don't all view it and take it seriously. Importance is subjective. *Lawrence of Arabia* is important to Stephen Spielberg. *Citizen Kane* is important to a world full of film makers. But not to me. *Pulp Fiction* is important to me because of the impact it made on me. It's no good telling me *2001:A Space Odyssey* is important if I'm never likely to watch it. I have done, by the way, but I don't really remember it.

Films are works of art, which means they can move you to tears, change your life, bore you, make you fall off your chair laughing, send you to sleep or have you stomping out of the cinema. But we are all so different, each person will have their own reaction, and one person's ground-breaking epic is another person's turgid turkey. So feel free to hold and express an opinion. Don't be swayed. If you love *Dirty Dancing 2, Jaws 3D* or *Death Wish 4*, then so be it. This is why I'm cautious about recommending films. And let me just say, the films in this book are not recommendations, they are just stories that have affected me in some way.

And so it is that I like *Evan Almighty*. And *Bruce Almighty* too. Not only are they entertaining comedies, but they also manage to throw difficult subject matter our way. *Bruce* is about what happens when you become successful and start to play God. And haven't we all done that from time to time. *Evan* is about what happens when faith and the demands of life make you look foolish and weaker. Or to put it another way, as the director Tom Shadyac described it, *Bruce* is about what happens when you get power, *Evan* is about what happens when you lose it. Whether or not you find these stories funny is just down to your sense of humour.

There are many great moments in both films. Like the time Bruce uses his power to part his soup, and God shows up with the line, 'Come, take a closer walk with me.' In other words following God is not so much about trying to get him to do powerful stuff, but rather getting to know him better. This was something that really began to matter to me, a few years back, as things fell apart and my life didn't seem to be about success so much anymore. My favourite *Bruce* moment is when he has fallen out with his girlfriend Grace, and cannot force her to love him. So Bruce does what God does, he leaves signs all over the place, telling Grace that he loves her. Reminding her on trees, in coffee shops, in songs and in the sky. This is often God's way. Some folks have a Damascus road experience from time to time, most of us get nudges and reminders in the ordinary and regular occurrences of life. Like Moses with that blazing wilderness bush, it's about noticing. Bushes regularly caught fire in that desert heat, but Moses drew closer and realised it was God speaking to him.

When Evan's wife Joan (of Ark) prays for their family to be closer together she bumps into God in the guise of a fast food waiter, who asks her whether God would answer such a prayer by making the family closer, or by giving them opportunities for that to happen. It's a hard question. We would all like God to change us and tricky situations for the better with the snap of a finger. And there are times when miracles like this do seem to happen. But often God works through his weapon of choice. Humans. What did he tell Adam and Eve? Look after things for me. Make good choices and care about the world and everything in it. When my wife was pregnant for the first time we prayed for an easy birth. I asked for a self-cleaning baby too. ☺ We got neither – but what we did get was a kind and understanding Christian midwife to help Lynn through a lot of the birthing process.

Years earlier when I was driving on the M4 and accidentally hit the brake and accelerator at the same time, we shot off the motorway at great speed and ploughed up a steep bank. After much prevaricating and discussion we prayed for help. My friend and I were stuck and the van we were travelling in was perched at a very precarious angle. We got a miracle. In the shape of two cops who pulled up, joked that we couldn't park the thing there, and then talked my mate through reversing the van to safety. Some mornings when I wake up and feel the pressures of the day ganging up on me, it can be an email from a friend, or an online post that gives me strength and refocuses me on what matters.

People.

We can be the cause of so many problems. But we can also be the answer to someone's prayer.

Patch Adams & Mr Tom.

I seem to spend much of my time these days trying not to be a control freak. I tend to feel responsible for things and wind myself up into a frenzy trying to get those things right. Recently I have begun to wonder whether this goes back to an incident in a barn with a mouse, or rather an imagined mouse. I must have been about seven or eight at the time, and had gone round with a bunch of friends to a farm where one of them lived. We had been given free rein to throw ourselves around on a stack of straw bales, and there was a wonderful sense of joy and freedom about the experience. It didn't matter how much you rolled or jumped or tumbled, you wouldn't get hurt. Fantastic. Till someone mentioned that there would be mice nesting in the straw. I can still recall now that sudden change in everything, moving from freedom and laughter to a feeling that I must be really careful about where I put my hands. I was not a big fan of rodents (we have had guinea pigs at various stages but they are cuddly and don't count) and the thought of a mouse landing on me scared the Scooby Doo out of me. And so I moved in an instant from freedom to worry. And I think that sense has stayed with me. I have to get things right or something might go terribly wrong.

Just last night (on this day of writing) I had a strange dream, in which I attended a kind of ramshackle conference with no agenda. We just wandered along to meetings, or gatherings, unsure of why we were there and what would happen. And though at first this all seemed odd, little by little it became more and more liberating.

There were no demands, no expectations, you could just wander about and enjoy being, rather than doing. Nothing needed to be achieved, there was no fear of something going wrong, I had nothing to control. It was an odd experience but it began to grow on me. I had to move from one mindset to another. It was disconcerting yet liberating and life-giving. It makes me think that it's not so much what we do, but our attitude as we do it. It's my attitude that frequently stresses me. I just need to push that magic button and reboot my approach to life.

I now have a version of asthma, called cough-variant, and I notice that it tends to spark up when I get stressed about doing things. Don't get me wrong, I'm grateful for my ability to organise, make things happen, spark things off. But everything has a shadow side and I guess I hold on too tightly at times, try to make too many things be exactly *right*.

And so to *Patch Adams*. Or rather one particular scene. Patch, a trainee doctor, loses his girlfriend, and walking to the edge of a cliff he wonders about throwing himself off. He starts to talk to God, questioning him, pouring out his frustration, pain and loss. Throwing back at God all the troubles that are wrecking his life. And then he spots a butterfly. A sign of rebirth, of new life. And a creature that his girlfriend loved. And suddenly he senses hope and steps back from the cliff edge. It's as if God answers his prayer with the arrival of that beautiful, colourful butterfly. I love that scene, and once, after watching it at Lee Abbey (we worked there from 2002 to 2011) I went outside and just soaked up the beauty and the sunshine and the wonder of the place. And felt just a little bit free. It's hard to put into words, but that new-found sense of life that Patch encountered seemed to bleed into me a little, and it led me outside, and for a while, helped me to let go a bit. Caught up in God's gift of the moment I felt, for a short while anyway, free. Running about on that field like a wonderfully random lunatic. A tad undignified perhaps, but liberating

I'm also reminded of the end of the TV film *Goodnight Mister Tom*, a moving story about William, a young boy evacuated to the countryside in World War Two, who goes to live with the grumpy but kind-hearted Mr Tom. As William comes hurtling down the hill on his bike, with the wind blowing in his smiling face, yelling 'Yaaaaaayyyyy!' he sees Mr Tom waiting for him at the bottom of the hill and instinctively calls out, for the first time, 'I can ride Dad! I can really ride!' The surprise and joy of that moment is captured on Tom's face as he hears William call him Dad.

It's another scene of healing and freedom and wonder. And a boy finding love and laughter with his new and good father. It sums up for me those moments when you rediscover that, as the writer Adrian Plass puts it, 'God is nice and he likes me.' Or to paraphrase the wonderful invitation from Song of Songs chapter 2 and verse 14, 'Come out from behind your rock, let me see you and hear you, for I love your face, and I love your voice.'

It's not about trying to please God by achieving lots of good things or avoiding all the bad things. But something else entirely. God wants to see us and hear us, he wants us to laugh and cry out, 'I can ride Dad! I can really ride!' Or to revisit another deeply moving scene in *The Railway Children*, when Bobby sees her father disembark from the train, she calls out, 'Daddy, my daddy!' Beautiful. Moves me to tears even as I describe it here now.

That's the wonder of films for me. Scenes about a heartbroken trainee doctor... and a damaged, fragile child... and a hopeful, devoted daughter can shout as loud as any sermon about the nature of a caring God, about his longing to be with us and to help us as we struggle.

Jaws.

In 1976 there was an explosion in cinema. Not the kind you now see accompanied by dropkicking superheroes and great balls of fire, a more subtle one. The motion pictures – they were a-changing. The arrival of a great white shark with its very own chilling soundtrack, 'Doo doo, doo doo, doo doo, doo doo...' meant just one thing. The blockbuster had been born. Mr Spielberg's legacy had landed. We didn't know it at the time of course. Back then we just saw *that* poster.

Oh that *poster*. That's really what I remember. It was everywhere. On the sides of cinemas, on advertising boards, and on the cover of Peter Benchley's book. Wondrously chilling. That massive, mysterious fish, with its jaws open wide as it swam up towards the unsuspecting body of that late night swimmer. Nowadays I have it on a t-shirt, a second t-shirt actually, as I wore the first one out. Back then I drew my own parody on the cover of an exercise book. A big fish swimming towards the surface with a gaping mouthful of... yes... *Gums.*

It also features one of my favourite lines of dialogue: 'You're gonna need a bigger boat.' As said by police chief Brody when he sees the size of the shark attempting to swallow them. Apparently Roy Schneider made up the line whilst they were filming. It's a scene I've called on sometimes when referencing the two miraculous and massive catches of fish that the disciples have with Jesus. The first one happens when they meet Jesus after a night of empty nets, the other takes place three years later, after the resurrection. The size of each catch is indeed so hefty that they look like needing bigger nets *and* boats. Real lottery-winning kind of hauls. So big that each catch would feed their families for a good while, thus freeing up the fishermen on both occasions. Firstly so they could leave their nets and go with Jesus for a while, and later to lead the newly formed church. Jesus knows everyone needs to live. He understands what it is to struggle to get by, and if these folk are to spend time following him then their families will need feeding for a while. The fish could be sold and the money then used for provisions.

I think I have misunderstood the miracles over the years, seeing them as Jesus 'proving' he is the Son of God. He never needed to do that in the way I perceived, which is why he wouldn't play along with the temptations in the wilderness, leaping off temples and turning stones to bread. When he did make miracle bread he began from a point of compassion. He saw the crowds and knew they would be hungry. Wondered how to help them. He understands that people grow weary and need food. We find that same principal when Elijah runs away into the desert, in 1 Kings 19. An angel shows up and tells him to eat something to restore his strength. Many of Jesus's miracles spring from a bigger picture too – from the panoramic canvas of the Old Testament. Elijah and Elisha both raise the dead. Elijah in 1 Kings 17 v 17, and Elisha in 2 Kings 4 v 32. In Isaiah 25 the prophet promises that God will feed his people, and so here comes Jesus throwing the biggest picnics and cooking breakfast on the beach. Moses took command over the sea in the daring escape from Egypt. Jesus calmed storms and walked on water. He was showing the people that he was following in the line of these great prophets, and at the same time, showing he was he was so much more.

When Jesus turned water into wine in John 2, he did it quietly. Not trying to announce or 'prove' anything, but rather responding to a need, and demonstrating the nature and desire of God to bring change and quality to life. I could go on, I often do, the point is that there are layers to these miracle stories. One last thought on Jesus feeding 5000 and 4000 people. These people normally would not eat together, they were from different levels of society. Here Jesus is throwing a banquet for all. Inviting them into this kingdom where everyone is welcome. Sinners and prostitutes, the sick and the healthy, the religious leaders and the tax collectors. The weak and the strong, the wise and the foolish. The women who will follow him to death and the fishermen who will run and hide. He is demonstrating the nature of God's kingdom breaking into this world, compassionate, welcoming, radical, counter-cultural, and life-changing. Offering everyone a new way to live.

Inspired by the poster I mentioned earlier I recently scribbled the following.

Jaws for Thought [a tail of something or nothing]

The great fish moved silently though the dark waters. He had read that opening line at the young age of 12 and had always feared the sea. And great fish. And so he stands here now, overwhelmed by this iconic poster, with the mouth of that great fish moving silently towards the pale body splashing its way noisily through the inky ocean. In the gloom. With the lights out and the dawn too far away. Who knows how long it will take that great fish to strike that vulnerable figure and pull it down into the dark waters? And with the fragility of things as they are, and the vulnerable nature of life as he knows it, how long before he meets a great fish in dark waters? 'Oops! Sorry love!' In his rush to escape his fate he bumps into a woman loaded with a tray of something packed in ice. No doubt heading for the market. 'I always thought he looked a bit fake,' she says, nodding towards the poster. 'In the film I mean. A bit cardboard. You should try some.' *Sorry?* he says. She holds up the glistening tray. 'It's delicious.' *What is?* he says. 'Shark! It's great! And jolly pleasing to turn the tables on the pesky thing for once.'

A kind of parable really, about the overwhelming nature of fear, and the way others can often help to burst the bubble of terror. When I was concocting it my family chatted about the way that friends can sometimes pull the rug on the fears that threatens us. Bring some perspective.

The Commitments & The Future.

Some films just set you buzzing. Make you feel alive. Whilst on a seven-week wander around South Africa I met up with an old friend who took me along to see *Back to the Future Part 2*. In a packed cinema. I had already been truly overwhelmed by what I had seen of Africa, not least that bus ride down the Garden Route from Durban to Port Elizabeth, now here I was hurled into a technicolour world of flying cars and hoverboards. It was happy and glorious. One of those evenings that will stay with me. Rich had been a great friend in my first spell at Lee Abbey (1984-1988) so spending a few days with him in Port Elizabeth was such a gift. I remember him killing a spider in the bath with his shoe, the thing was so big it split apart and the hefty body flew in two directions. We also bought pizzas that BTF2 night which were so big we were eating them for the next week. They were like tractor wheels, but I digress...

A year or so later I went with some friends to see the film which for years has hovered on the brink of being my all-time favourite movie. We missed *The Commitments* when it first came out but caught it on a late night re-release after it won the Bafta for best picture in 1991. It's about a group of friends in Dublin who form a soul band, argue a lot, and sing their sweet and ragged hearts out to classics like *Try a Little Tenderness, Midnight Hour* and *Mustang Sally.* I've never quite been able to put my finger on what it is about that film, but after we saw it the first time I was buzzing for days. It seemed, I suppose, so full of life and humour and friendship, a tale of battling against the odds. I'll be honest, the dialogue is ripe and the characters are rough and ready. But that's the point really. It's rooted in reality. I wouldn't be surprised if the friends Jesus picked were not unlike this. Young soul punks, with true grit in their DNA, ready to take on the world. Not your typical heroes, but mavericks unafraid of the glowering goliaths and frothing behemoths out there. *They had absolutely nothing, but they were willing to risk it all* the swaggering poster declared. The performances drip with sweat and self-belief, and the well-worn songs tell stories of struggle and survival.

Another film that set me buzzing was the animated comedy, *Captain Underpants*. I know, who'd have thought that. I'd seen the trailer and noticed the anarchic and chaotic humour and so went racing for the picture house with our older daughter as soon as it arrived. Did we enjoy it? Does the captain wear underpants? We laughed our... well I won't say underpants off but certainly our socks off. I'm not a fan of animated films but when something as daft as this comes along I find it irresistible. Afterwards, as I wandered into our local supermarket, I was busting to tell someone... anyone... that I'd just seen *Captain Underpants*. They'd have thought me mad, so I didn't do it. But part of me still wishes I had. The experience had been so much fun. And laughter is such great medicine. Those endorphins were going bananas inside me. I just felt so good.

Good funny stories are like gold dust. Jesus knew that. Which is why he told so many of them. Sadly we don't think of the parables as funny. Because we think Holy stories must be serious. But in his day Jesus's tales would have lit up the smiles and brought forth the guffaws. They upended the po-faced religion of his day and challenged the damaging ideas that prevailed. These days when I talk about TV remotes down the back of the sofa you can see the audience break into a corporate smile. Been there done that. Well, that's exactly how it would have been when Jesus told his tale of a farmer hunting high and low for his sheep. And his yarn about the woman turning her furniture upside-down to find that missing thruppenny bit. Everyone knew what it was like to be turning the place on its head, and everyone still does. Car keys and mobile phones and the prodigal things of our day. We may foam at the mouth at the time, but afterwards they make great social media posts. 'Like' this post if you've ever lost your nose stud in the loo, or in the dog, or up your nose. These are shared stories, memorable, repeatable, viral. And when they become a hook for a facet of the kingdom of God... well all the better. The God who hunts high and low for us, the God who delves into the darkness and the grit, and the grimy cobwebbed recesses to bring us back.

So his stories were doubly good. They were loaded with puns and humour, AND they led you right back to God's front door. God's wide open and welcoming front door. Shocking and sensational. They would have had people buzzing for days.

That Thing You Do.

When Gandalf the Grey (last seen falling to his destruction in *The Fellowship of the Ring*) reappeared as Gandalf the White in the second LOTR movie, *The Twin Towers*, I thought something like, 'Oh well, he's okay now, they can't kill him, he's already been to death and back.' And there was a feeling that all threat to him was now lifted.

Which may well have been what Jesus's mates felt about him once the resurrection had finally sunk in. They couldn't do anything to Jesus now, they can't get rid of him, he's already been to death and back. They can make jokes, spread rumours, intimidate and ridicule his friends, or come up with smart putdowns. But they can't dispose of him. Not anymore.

Many films feature resurrection moments, scenes when what seemed lost is rediscovered. Hope returns, a relationship is restored, an enemy overcome, a life changed. But for my money, nothing is better than the moment the Wonders hear their single on the radio for the first time. That may not sound ground-breaking, but it's their reaction which beats everything. *That Thing You Do* is both the title of the Wonders' first record (a 45 – remember those?) and also the title of the film. The Wonders are a small local Pennsylvania band, desperate to have some success. So they record a single and send it to the local radio station, wondering if it will ever be played. Then Faye, girlfriend of the lead singer, goes to post a few letters (posting letters – remember them??) and is stopped in her tracks as she hears the song announced on her portable transistor. (Remember those???) She runs like blazes to find the others as the track plays, gathering the group from various locations until they all wind up in the local electrical store, dancing like lunatics as the song blasts out from the great big wireless radio. (Remember them???) It's a glorious few minutes, the celebration building as the song plays and the jubilance grows. You can't help but feel good and I wondered whether those first disciples, that group of courageous women, experienced that kind of exuberant joy after meeting Jesus on that unexpectedly hopeful Sunday.

I doubt if the men danced. Not that morning anyway. It took them a while to venture out and they had to wait for Sunday evening before they had their first meet-up with the risen Son. But perhaps, when the others weren't looking, they did a little secret jig. Or a bit of the twist. Or the mashed potato. I'm sure Andrew would have. And maybe young John Mark too. There is a lovely scene in *50 First Dates* when a love struck Henry does a secret dance behind a parked truck, only to be revealed when the truck unexpectedly pulls away. Maybe Simon Peter did that. Leapt around behind the chariot sheds. I hope so. The resurrection should make us fizz a little bit. On the inside anyway. Even if we don't dance.

Gladiator.

'Today I know that the experiences of our lives, when we let God use them, become the mysterious and perfect preparation for the work he will give us to do.'

So said the great Corrie Ten Boom, and I see now, looking back, how well that describes my eighteen months working in a cinema in Woking. Those days when I felt so out of my depth, perpetually embarrassed because everyone else was younger and cooler than me. A little afraid I would say or do the wrong thing. Wondering where I was heading, if I was actually heading anywhere at all, and whether there would ever be a new start for me.

In the middle of each cinema shift we were allowed a twenty minute break, and when I first started I wondered what I'd do with it. On one occasion I wandered around the nearby library but that didn't really cut the mustard. It took a little while for the penny to drop. I could go into one of the screens and watch part of a film! This was the dream part of the job for me. I got to watch free films, admittedly in twenty minute or half hour chunks, but still. Movies movies movies. So I used my break times to do that. And watched loads of films. At the end of each late shift, once we had cleaned up, we had to go and sit in on an allocated screen for the last part of the late night film. Again. A dream come true. On one all day shift I managed to watch an entire film, going in each showing to watch a different twenty minutes. What you might call jigsaw movie watching.

Oh and just to go off at a tangent here... discussing this book with my wife, and trying to figure out a title, she told me that the early descriptive name of 'moving pictures' got abbreviated two ways. In the USA it became 'movies', in the UK – 'the pictures'. Just a bit of trivia for you, no one walks away from this book empty-handed!

When moving pictures hit their 100th birthday, the cinemas around the UK celebrated by offering showings for a £1 a go. We couldn't resist it and went to see a couple of films that day. A matinee showing of the rom-com *One Day* starring George Clooney and Michelle Pfeiffer, (the first time I'd seen mobile phones feature heavily in a storyline, as the two fractious stars did battle with their chaotic day and one another); and the gloriously over-the-top 'convicts on a plane' romp *Con Air* with Nic Cage and a whole bunch of crooks and tough guys. We loved both movies but especially *Con Air*, which never took itself too seriously, and which seemed so big it leapt off the screen and into your lap at times.

On the subject of mobile phones, it was whilst working in the cinema that I first encountered texting. I remember a group of us gathering around one of the young female staff members as she showed us this strange and wonderful experience. You could type into your phone! For 10p a time! How novel. Surely it wouldn't last.

One of the key experiences that stayed with me from those days, happened the night *Gladiator* was released. At the time I had never heard of it, but that quickly changed. I was tearing tickets on a long walkway towards the screens and I recall very clearly watching this massive bunch of guys head towards me down the wide corridor. They had all come to see this sword and sandal epic. And later, when I had watched the film myself (probably in twenty minute chunks) it struck me that we have a Bible chock full of these kinds of tales of courage, catastrophe and grit; epic stories of people doing battle with wild animals, enemies and events that have turned against them. Surely we could tell those tales in such a way that it might just appeal to some of the guys who had come to see Maximus Decimus Meridius? When I wrote *The Bloke's Bible* a few years later I reckon that experience shaped my approach to rewriting biblical scenes.

One of the first pieces I wrote which ended up in *The Bloke's Bible* was inspired by something else, a fantastic slab of writing in Frederick Buechner's book *Telling the Truth*. He wonderfully describes the Roman governor Pilate with yellowed fingertips from smoking too much, setting him in a modern pulp fiction kind of context. Pilate has decided to give up the ciggies, his throat dry and his chest raw from too many. He is driven to work in a limo, and has to deal with various problems. There is an epidemic amongst the slaves in the city, the tax people are not doing their job properly. And now here is Jesus, standing in front of his desk, his face swollen from a beating, as Pilate quizzes him about truth. He stayed up late last night talking politics and would like to give this unwashed prisoner the carfare home. Plus his wife called earlier on the phone, tearful after another difficult night and having had some bad dream. I love the way Buechner unashamedly messes with time, taking the bones of the story and dropping them smack into another time, another context. And so I wrote this piece...

The sun rises on another day, blinking intermittently through the straggling lines of bulging grapes. The owner rises too, sits up and stretches. He reaches for his first cup of coffee, brought to him at the ringing of a distant bell. He sits on the gleaming white veranda and enjoys the first dark taste of steaming caffeine as he watches the children running barefoot in the olive groves below. The day looks like another warm one, the skyline is blue and clear. Beneath him, in the many bedrooms of his sprawling home, his family stirs after another night of partying. The sons he is so proud of, the daughters he treasures and protects. The grandchildren, who make him laugh so heartily, continue to run amok in the fields, doing more damage than good, but he does not mind; he has many more fields, only a limited number of grandchildren. Their happiness and well-being mean more than a thousand acres of well-kept land. Their cheerful freedom is worth its weight in golden barley.

A servant appears in the yard below, and the two exchange a few words, the master bestowing the day's doings upon the faithful butler, more a friend than a serf. Half an hour wanders lazily by and the family assembles for breakfast alfresco, a starched white table laid with the produce of goodness and mercy. There is much laughter, yawning, fresh fruit and warm bread. The children wrestle with their parents and the parents wrestle with each other. Their words tussle and their jokes jostle for first place, but the meaning is amicable.

More servants pass by, dragging bulky oxen and pompous horses. A few clouds saunter past, pausing long enough to admire the landscape before wandering off in search of more turbulent scenes to rain upon. The family makes their many plans, which include another party soon. They chart their summer and plot the farming months ahead. The grapes are looking good this year, the crop will be an extravagant one. The owner sits back and for a moment, just a moment, considers what life might be like if he were poor and alone. But his moment of consideration is a short one. He ponders for no more than a second, and then the morbid moment is gone.

Life is good. The future holds out a full fist of promise. He affords himself a smile, and his eldest son returns it. The day is a happy one, the man is mightily blessed. He is at one with the world and at peace with his God. His name is Job, and before the day is out, he will have lost everything.

I found a new freedom in exploring these stories in a context that messed up the old and the new. You could tell them in such a way that we might be there, sitting with Job in the sun, or passing nearby.

Gladiator was certainly one of those films which began this kind of rethink. And the seeds of that new approach began to grow in the scrub of that wilderness cinema time. Years before, when I saw *Reservoir Dogs* I had wondered then about how to communicate with the kind of guys that loved Tarantino but had no notion of Jesus. This kind of writing was my attempted response. (I began *The Bloke's Bible* with an account of some of the sex and violence in King David's life.)

One clip from *Gladiator* that I have used time and time again, has a certain Job-like quality. Maximus escapes wrongful imprisonment and flees from the evil Commodus, but on returning home he finds his farm devastated and his family destroyed. He falls to his knees in the dirt and collapses in his pain. He has lost everything. He lies there helpless and empty. A story that many resonate with, one way or another. There are many ways of losing everything, for myself I *felt* as if I had lost everything because I had no aspirations, no clear way forward, no plan or purpose. For so many, for far, far too many, it is about actually losing *everything*, through wars, riots, plagues, famines, earthquakes, oppression, invasion, first world greed... the list goes on. And so does the losing everything.

The Bible is full of people who are in some kind of trouble. Their stories, and their cries and prayers, are there for us. As we express our pain and the pain of the world. 'I believe, help my unbelief.' 'I'm sinking in deep mud.' 'My God, why have you forsaken me...' 'My pillow is soaked with my tears.' 'Why do the nations rage?' 'If only you'd been here...' Corrie Ten Boom experienced awful darkness in her life, with God's help in that darkness she was able to say, 'Love is larger than the walls which shut it in.'

Rob Bell writes that the Bible is true, not only because it happened, but because it continues to happen. Every day. For someone somewhere. These stories continue to play out. Adam and Eve being tempted, Abraham and Sara trekking into the unknown, Paul stopped in his tracks by an unexpected encounter on a Damascus Road,

Peter running for his life with his faith hidden under his clothes, Ruth and Naomi trudging along in their disappointment, Esther feeling out of her depth because too much is being asked of her, Mary finding unexpected encouragement from her cousin Elizabeth, Joseph wondering if his dreams will ever come true. These stories become our stories, and the writers of the Bible offer them to us, and the accounts of God with all these people, in their struggles and triumphs, in their questions and discoveries. Most of the characters in the Bible have messy, pressured lives. Their days are troubled and chaotic. And God is with them through it all.

I found that films helped me to explore these contradictions and questions, to be honest about my own struggles. Showing Maximus in his mess gave me the currency to be a little more honest about some of my own. I wasn't Job and I wasn't a gladiator, far from it! But we had a shared humanity. A common reality. Plus I was claiming to follow a man who is The Truth, a rescuer from Nazareth who spoke of reality setting us free. However, it's not always easy to let the truth out in Christian circles, because we expect a certain standard of ourselves. Now I was discovering that cinema was a device that helped me lower my guard a little, and an unexpected key to unlock and rediscover the meaning of that genuine truth and reality.

West Side Story.

I'm a sucker for a good tune. I love the *Gee, Officer Krupke* number from this film. Catchy and funny and full of great performances from these streetwise guys, as they sing about their woes. 'My parents treat me rough, with their marijuana, they won't give me a puff!' and 'I'm not anti-social, I'm just anti-work!' When I was at Lee Abbey we wrote a number based on the *La la la la la America* song – *La la la la la Lee Abbey*. The original has great lines, full of witty put-downs, as the girls and guys argue about the pluses and minuses of life in America. The guys sing about organised crime and a terrible time in America, but the girls gleefully reply, 'You forget **I'm** in America!' So we came up with a lively and tuneful argument between the guys and the girls on the community. Sadly, it never got performed. But it was fun coming up with the ideas. Apologies if it now seems sexist, it was of its time and full of good-natured banter between a male estate team and a female kitchen team. Brace yourself... oh and feel free to sing along:

Guys: Out on the estate it is so great,
Guys: No girls to give us a headache,
Guys: No women wailing and weeping!
Girls: No one to stop you from sleeping!

Guys: Plenty of work down in Lee Abbey.
Girls: Plenty of jerks down in Lee Abbey!
Guys: Plenty of perks down in Lee Abbey.
Girls: Nothing but squirts down in Lee Abbey!

Girls: In the kitchen it's sweet and we're such pearls!
Guys: Outside we are tough and there's no girls!
Girls: In the kitchen it's lonely with no men.
Guys: Then why don't you kidnap a chaplain!

Guys: We are the boys down in Lee Abbey.
Girls: Plenty of noise down in Lee Abbey!
Guys: We don't earn much down in Lee Abbey.
Girls: But you've got **US** down in Lee Abbey!

West Side Story reminds me of another film, a non-musical true story. One of the first faith-based movies I think. *The Cross and the Switchblade* is based on David Wilkerson's account of his call to reach out to the gangs of New York, and about some of the street kids who became Christians. There are no songs in this movie, but that same New York gang culture, with a different outcome. Nicky Cruz was one of those gang members, and his biography by Jamie Buckingham, *Run Baby Run*, is still one of my favourite books. It's a testimony book which has it all. Sex, violence, gangs, conversion, doubt, questions, disappointment and hope. It probably inspired some of my more gritty writing in *The Bloke's Bible*.

The actor and singer Pat Boon played David Wilkerson in the movie. Pat was already a Christian by then and apparently DW asked him to go away and pray for an encounter with the Holy Spirit before he played the part. It happened and the film has since had a significant impact down the years. My first powerful encounter with God's Spirit occurred on the same weekend that I first heard Fleetwood Mac's album *Rumours*. So that album is a useful reminder for me. You never know what songs, movies, TV programmes, jokes etc. can serve as a reminder of God's presence in your life.

Notting Hill.

'Could you adios these dirty dishes...'

It's a movie quote that sadly does not appear in those lists which usually include lines like,

'I could have been a contender.'

And 'Frankly my dear I don't give a damn!'

But it's a shame because I rather like it. It's a line written by Richard Curtis and delivered by Alec Baldwin in *Notting Hill*, in a scene where the hapless Will suddenly discovers that the love of his life, movie star Anna Scott, already has a brash and cocky American boyfriend. And it's this boyfriend who mistakes him for a hotel employee and asks him to tidy the room a bit and take out the trash.

Another favourite line comes from the scene where Anna is asking Will to love her. 'The fame thing isn't real you know...' she says, 'I'm just a girl, standing in front of a boy, asking him to love her.' See, I told you, she's asking him to love her. Believe it or not I once misquoted that about God. *Just God standing in front of people, asking them to love him.* Now as cheesy as that sounds, I think there's something profound about it. Religion can get very muddled and technical and theological and complex. But meet someone who hasn't been a Christian very long, as we did recently, and you're right back to that simple statement. It's about someone discovering the love of God. It's wonderfully disarming. Not about understanding him, or having all the answers, not about being able to argue your way out of a theological maze, or holding a bagful of smart answers. Just someone loving God. Even someone being *in love* with him. It can sound awfully simplistic to those of us who are, you know... experts at this Christian lark. ☺ But what did Jesus say to that bunch in Ephesus? You've lost your first love. Something that we probably all do from time to time. The baggage piles up. The pressures build. We become a little more 'mature'. *Just a God standing in front of people, asking them to love him.* I know. It sounds almost heretical doesn't it. We're talking about the Almighty here. The maker of heaven and earth. Are we allowed to say that he wants our love like that? Well, just take a look at a woman whose been dumped by five husbands, rejected, ignored, made to feel worthless. And then see her reaction after she has held an honest, searching, in-depth conversation with Jesus. What does she do? Stroll sedately back and write a book about how his theology has impressed her? No. She's chaotic, she's spilling out the news, her face is flushed, she's full of talk about meeting someone who knows all about her and doesn't reject her. Someone who accepts her. Understands her. Knows all about it. Almost like being in love.

That said, I do understand that following Jesus is about many things. It affects all of our being. Personally, I love discovering the layers to his conversations, stories, encounters and actions. I love finding out that there's a rich fool in the Old Testament called Nabal and just maybe Jesus got the idea for his rich fool story in Luke 12 from that. Or that the quote in Malachi 4 about 'the sun of righteousness rising with healing in his *wings*' may well have inspired the woman with bleeding to reach out and touch the hem of Jesus's robe in Mark 5, because the word for *wings* refers to the edge of a rabbi's tunic. There is so much to learn and discover in the Bible, so much to broaden and deepen our faith. And I know too that this love and dedication is not merely emotional – it involves our wills, minds, souls and strength. As well as our hearts. Many of us may never feel much at all about it. Emotions can trick us, they are overrated. But that simple devotion, that simple trust, present alongside all that life throws at us, helping us through. That's surely gold dust. Just this week I heard an astonishing story in an online sermon. A group of South Korean missionaries were kidnapped by the Taliban and brutally mistreated. Two of them were executed. Then, after they were released several of them spoke about wishing they were still prisoners. They had felt so close to Jesus in that terrible situation, and were struggling to sense that closeness again now that they had been freed. What an extraordinary situation. I can hardly get my head around it. But that sense of Jesus was so close, so intimate, in that awful experience.

In my own experience I have known times when I have sensed him near in a gentle affirming way, sensed his care, his warmth and acceptance. Just a gentle experience. Hard to put on the page. To describe it in mere words. On one occasion it came about through reading the verse from Song of Songs chapter 2 and verse 14. And since then that sense of God's love has remained with me. It's a very precious thing for which I am extremely grateful.

To finish, another Richard Curtis quote, this one from *Love Actually*. 'Life is full of interruptions and complications.' Jesus made opportunities out of interruptions and complications. I just get frustrated. So much to learn. So much to learn.

The Untouchables.

Years before I ever began drawing on films for reflections on life and faith a couple of moments from this movie stuck in my mind. Simple moments really. It's set in the days of the mobsters, and treasury agent Elliot Ness is dead set on catching Al Capone and bringing his Chicago empire crashing down. One morning Elliot's wife packs up his lunch, and taking a piece of paper to wrap up some carrot sticks, she scribbles a short message of love on it. Later when Elliot is sitting in his car eating his lunch he opens the packet, looks at his partner and says, 'Nice to be married.' Films do that a lot. Sum up a world of thought in a few simple words and gestures. They pare down a lot of info into a few seconds, and that's why it's good to watch them more than once. There is so much going on. Nothing on screen happens by chance, it's all there for a reason. The other moment was when Elliot looks across the room at his young daughter and waggles his finger at her in a subtle mini-wave. I like that. I still sometimes use that mini-wave.

There are of course loads of great moments, not least the pivotal shootout in Union railway station. Inspired by a similar scene in the 1925 epic Battleship Potemkin, a mother accidentally lets her pram run down the endless steps as cops and gangsters shoot at one another around it. The baby coos and the mother screams as the pram clunks step by step towards destruction in slow motion. In the end it is only saved by Andy Garcia, as one of Ness's untouchable cops, jamming his foot under the wheel just in the nick of time. When I first watched that it really was jaw dropping and it stayed with me for a long time.

But the first scene I referenced came from the time Elliot goes round to ask beat cop Malone (an Irish cop with a Scottish accent played by the great Sean Connery) if he will join his small band of good men. Malone says he wishes Ness had come sooner, when he was younger and thinner. 'So,' he says, 'thank you, no.' I couldn't help but think on Moses, who had once wanted to change the world but was now out in the desert tending sheep and keeping his head down. The day that bush burned really set the cat among the pigeons for him. He says, 'Thank you, no,' a good few times. But of course, like Malone, ends up doing the job. I felt a strange affinity towards Moses, because when things fell apart for us, and the wheels came off the drama and mime ministry I had been doing, I felt as if I'd wandered into a desert and maybe all the good days were gone.

In another scene that I love, Malone takes Ness round to the police training college so he can recruit more help. Malone tells him that if he wants a healthy apple he shouldn't go to the barrel, but instead pick it off the tree. In other words get a fresh cop who is as yet untainted by the corrupt system. I refer to this when talking about Jesus's unusual procedure for choosing disciples. He bypassed the religious systems of his day and instead went to men and women who had not been tainted and misled by the wrong kind of teaching and thinking. Men and women who were not thought of as good spiritual material. They would never have been chosen to be scribes or Pharisees or priests. (Especially not the women! No chance! They were just second-class citizens.) Yet Jesus heads straight for them. He wants good apples, and he knows where to find them. Not perfect or flawless people. But full of potential, and hungry for the right kind of change.

There are of course memorable scenes (this one in a church) where it is advisable not to take the advice literally! Malone is certainly wholehearted and wants Elliot to be the same. 'What are you prepared to do? He pulls a knife, you pull a gun. He puts one of your men in the hospital, you put one of his in the morgue. That's the Chicago way.' The Nazarene's way was also wholehearted, but totally the opposite of this, service not violence, peace rather than a gun, and another kind of victory altogether. There are not many films which highlight the power of choosing the way of peace. *Hotel Rwanda* comes to mind. And *Schindler's List*. And *Gandhi* of course. But more on that later.

When *The Untouchables* was given a cinematic re-release in the early 90s I encouraged a bunch of good friends to go along for a late night showing. I was desperate to see it again on the big screen. I don't recall the others being quite as impressed as I was, but that's films for you. 50% is what happens on that screen, 70% is about your own experience and personality and what's going on in your head. And I know that doesn't add up, but it's my book. ☺

Truman & Groundhog Day.

During lockdown one film has been referenced time and again. Yes. *Groundhog Day.* Each day has seemed so similar that we have felt caught up in the same 24 hours over and over again. There is a moment in the film when Phil tells a local guy that every day is the same and he feels trapped. 'I know what you mean,' the local guy mutters back. And that's the core of the movie. Anyone can feel caught in a life which is going round and round. With no hint of moving forward. And where's the meaning in that?

I believe the idea for this story came to the writer when he was reading about vampires. He was thinking about what it must be like to be stuck in a particular kind of life. One going on forever. Or I may have just made all that up! Apologies if so. Anyway, the final film has cynical TV presenter Phil trapped in the snowy town of Punxsutawney, living the same day over and over again. Each morning he wakes to the same song and the same radio banter. The same people say the same things to him and he is expected to report (yet again, and again, and again...) on the appearance, or not, of the groundhog creature, to signify whether spring is on the way. Apparently, if you have the time to work it out, Phil ends up trapped in Punxsutawney, reliving the same day, for more than 10,000 days! The question is, will Phil get wiser without getting older?

If I were trapped in the same day, where nothing I did had any lasting value or repercussion, I'll be honest, I wouldn't mind robbing a bank. Not really for the money, but for the dangerous thrill of it. No one would get hurt, I promise, it would all be very well-meaning (I'd probably say 'please' a lot of times) and if I got shot or arrested, well, I'd wake up in the same bed hearing the same song on the radio all over again. Because nothing changes in Groundhog land.

As the story develops Phil chooses to use his time more creatively. He learns to play the piano, and regularly repeats the same helpful tasks for those around him. He knows that a certain boy will fall from the tree at that particular moment. He knows that tyre will burst and need fixing. So he is ready. And day after day he does these same things. But he is changing as he does it. He is no longer the cynical, selfish guy he was when he arrived in Punxsutawney. I remember thinking that if I was trapped in the same day I might learn the piano. Which is a little daft because you don't have to be stuck in Punxsutawney to learn new skills and change a little. When lockdown first started in March 2020 we did make a change for the better, we began working out with Joe Wicks on YouTube. I hasten to add we weren't with him on YouTube. That would be a terrible thought. But for a few months we took a few moments in the day to get fitter. Then lockdown changed and our lives shifted a little. Slowly Joe slipped away into the shadows. I had also picked up my daughter's ukulele when we were confined indoors, and for a while I strummed a little and learned a few chords. But time has passed and I still can't play it. Lasting change is not easy.

Truman is not trapped in the same day, but he is shackled within his own show. He doesn't know it but his life is merely a massive film set, and millions are watching what he does. His relationships, his job, his home life and leisure, everything is orchestrated by the director Christof. A God-like figure who watches from afar and manipulates Truman for his own ends. I have heard that this film is about the movie industry itself, and there is a hint when a Dalmatian appears at one point, growling, fangs bared. Not a happy, cuddly Disney creature, but a predator. *La La Land* is certainly about the industry, and the struggle between success and affirmation. But more on that later.

What we can say is that we now might feel as if we are all living in our own Truman shows. Observed. Our lives publicised and analysed. But unlike Truman we have brought that on ourselves. We have embraced social media and in doing so created our own version of Christof. We are Big Brother watching ourselves. Analysing one another, criticising, wrong-calling each other. Hampering each other's growth and movement. We are now cautious, frightened even, of our own opinions, just in case they don't fall in line with popular opinion, and someone innocently retweets them and someone else then turns them into accusations. Father forgive us, for we don't know what we're doing. Free speech seems to be shuffling ever closer to death's doorstep. And we have brought it on ourselves. We have perhaps been too quick to broadcast on social media the kind of things we used to mutter to ourselves when stuck in traffic. Or perhaps rumour-monger over the fence to a neighbour. Now the garden fence is global. And, to misquote Jesus, what we whisper on Twitter might well be shouted from the digital rooftops.

But to more hopeful things. Christof has created Truman (no accident that he is called a True-man) in the image of your average and relatively innocent person. But Christof has himself been created in the image of a self-absorbed and misguided God. A controlling being, who pulls Truman's strings and hoicks him here and there. Truman might think he is the captain of his soul, but it's not so. And where does that leave us?

Well, discussing it for one thing. Is there a God who is controlling and manipulative like that? Or is there a God who has given us the gift of freewill? A gift which means we don't live in Truman's bright and cheery and litter-free world. Instead we live in a place where trouble and joy both stalk the streets. As Jesus once said, wheat and weeds grow alongside each other. For now. That's our world. And I believe we have a God who is interested and understanding and wanting to be involved as we make our freewill choices. Truman overcomes his fear of water to sail to the edge of his limited world, can be seen bashing on the fabricated horizon. Will he go beyond this situation of unreality and control? Break free from the idea of a God who is distorting his worldview? Of course he will (this is a comedy after all) – he'll walk free. And there's a final and somewhat profound comment about all those faithful viewers who love Truman and his life. The moment the show is over... they switch to another channel. What else is out there to entertain them?

And to just put that for a moment in *Groundhog Day* terms. I guess if Phil was spending his endless days watching Truman, feeling ever more trapped in his own show, then gradually, as his 10,000+ days roll by, Phil doesn't merely switch channels. He turns his TV off. And to misquote the title of an old kids TV show – he *Goes Off To Do Something Less Boring Instead.*

La La Land.

This best-picture-Oscar-winner-for-two-minutes will always hold a special place in my heart. It taught me so much about digging deeper into a film. When I first saw it (whilst working as a projectionist in a nearby cinema) I did not get it at all. Not one bit. And I had heard such wonderful things. Awards. Accolades. Speeches. Applause. It had burst through the cinematic gates at the start of 2017 and blown the competition right out of the water. *Here's to the fools who dream.* The poster declared, and there were Emma Stone and Ryan Gosling in yellow, black and white set against a twinkling, blue night sky. So what had I missed? Clearly Emma and Ryan were not Fred and Ginger. And this musical odyssey was not *Singing in the Rain.* So what was it? I went home, and as we do these days, I Googled and YouTubed. And everything began to change. I recommend doing a bit of research on films you have enjoyed, or not, it's fascinating to read about the stories behind them, and the messages hidden between the lines. Of course *La La Land* wasn't *Singing in the Rain.* It was never meant to be, it just drew on the same sensibilities, with a rather different intention. The title should have warned me. *La La Land.* A bonkers place. Where people are doolally. The opening scene says it all, lots of shiny people singing about another day of sun – and stuck in traffic. Stuck. Going nowhere.

Mia wants to be a famous and successful actress. But like so many wannabes she serves coffee all day. Sebastian plays piano in a club that won't let him perform the jazz he loves. Both are desperate to break out. It's all kind of summed up in one of the songs. *City of Stars.* When Sebastian first sings this he is looking longingly at tinsel town, wondering whether he will ever make it. Whether his dreams are little more than dust. A mirage which will never morph into reality. But when he duets the song with Mia later, they sing of other things. Will they be loved? Will they have someone who says to them I'm here and you'll be all okay. They sing of being in the bars and the crowded restaurants, but needing something more. Something about affirmation, something beyond their dreams coming true.

They are of course falling in love with each other, and that path will not be a smooth one. Before long the potholed road of success will cause both of them to stumble. What will become of them? And their 'city of stars' dreams? There is a telling moment early on when Mia serves coffee to a famous movie star. We don't know who it is because we barely set eyes on them. Mostly we see their feet, and Mia's reaction. And this is the point. This is a clue to what the future might hold. This movie star is not a person, not to Mia anyway, she is merely a famous name who can get free coffee. She has ceased to be a cherished individual.

When Mia and Sebastian first dance together Mia very obviously removes her high heels and puts on flat shoes. Because that's reality. Ginger Rogers once said that in their routines she did everything Fred Astaire did, but backwards and in high heels. Well, Mia is a real person, not yet famous, not successful in Hollywood terms, so she will dance in flat shoes. The camera pans up from their routine, gives us a long, loving look at the horizon then drifts down again. It struck me as odd when I first saw it. Well, in those old movies when the camera panned up, hovered for a moment, and then came down again, whilst it was away the costumes and the scenery would magically have changed, glammed up. But not here. Nothing changes. Mia and Sebastian are just dancing in the street. Not far from their parked cars. And their routine will end when they are interrupted by Mia's phone. Not very Fred and Ginger at all.

So I reckon that Damien Chazelle's film is all about the tussle between stardom, glitz and humanity. What Hollywood can do to you, and what people really need. We all crave fame and success, we long to be affirmed and know that we are all right. We are, after all, none of us normal, and all of us unique. Though we may do our best to cover our tracks. *Why blend in when you were made to stand out?* I really like that line, it was on a card I was once given. I love that, and aspire to it, but I know at times that I try to blend in because I don't want to be misunderstood or belittled for being different.

In the end I saw *La La Land* four times – I did lots of projectionist shifts while it was showing. And every time I saw more in it. Films can be like that, holding many pearls of wisdom that are not at first evident. Like Jesus's parables. The prodigal son is like *La La Land* in that way, full of layers and insights that lie beneath the surface. I wrote about it once on my website. In fact, if you keep reading, it's the next chapter. ☺

La La Layers & The Prodigal.

Jesus's tales were full of la la layers, and can be received in all kinds of ways. On the one hand the prodigal son tale is about a wayward brother, and the welcoming generosity and forgiveness of his father. On the other hand it's about an older brother in a very dangerous position because, unlike his younger brother, he doesn't realise he is lost. He thinks he's fine thanks. And even goes so far as to thoroughly insult his father by sounding off at his dad and refusing to come to the welcome home party.

The prodigal's brother should have gone looking for his younger sibling. It was his job to rescue him. But he was having none of it. Preferring instead to judge and criticise him. It was easier to point the finger than offer a helping hand. So there is actually a third son in the story – or rather a third son *telling* the story. The older brother stands there with folded arms and a scowl on his face. So Jesus has come instead to look for the lost and to rescue them.

Peel another layer and you find a retelling of the story of Jacob and Esau, and a prodigal Jacob returning home not filthy rich and married with children, but filthy having wasted everything on parties. He does not have the credentials to prove himself, but instead has the obvious need for a higher, generous grace.

Peel again and we find a father who runs to protect his son from the rest of the community, hell-bent on stoning him to death, because there is a law about punishing a wayward teenager, to make an example of him. (In Deuteronomy 21 v 18-21 there is the rather shocking instruction about this.) The father therefore runs to wrap himself around the boy, so that he himself will receive any punishing blows. A foreshadowing of the punishment Jesus took on the cross for every lost person.

The father's compassion in this way gives a deeper meaning to his words to the older brother. 'He was declared dead,' the father says at the end of the tale, 'but not by me – I never wrote him off – he is alive!' The father believes in resurrection. He sees beyond our mistakes, our failures, our catastrophes and slip-ups. He sees a new beginning, a thousand new beginnings. For us. In Jesus. The prodigal rescuer.

'Here's to the hearts that ache... here's to the mess we make,' sings Mia in La La Land; yes, and here's to the one who understands all this, knows what we yearn for, and waits for us to turn so he can come running, with his bag of second chances. La la layers, worth peeling back.

Ferris Bueller.

I came to *Ferris Bueller's Day Off* late. My wife
Lynn had been watching it since the 1980s. It
has since become one of the go-to movies in our
house, as our older daughter Amy loves it too.
Ferris decides he'll take a day out of school and
persuades his mate Cameron and girlfriend Mia
to join him. He feigns illness, something his
sister does not swallow for one second, and once
his parents have gone out he leaps up, dresses
down and pretends to be Mia's dad so he can
take her out of school for a family funeral.
Obviously one should never bunk off school for
any reason, although I think I did once or twice. I
seem to remember slipping into a pub on a cross
country run once, although goodness knows how
we got drinks, at sixteen I looked about twelve. I
recently read that Bear Grylls' dad told him,
'Don't peak at school or you'll mess up the rest of
your life.' Ferris would agree with that.

Anyway, much cavorting is had, and because
this is a feelgood 80s teen flick it's all larger than
life and full of colour and music. A day the rest of
us can only dream about. And of course, being a
movie about teenagers this is also a coming of
age yarn. Something the movies revisit again and
again. The Bible is full of those too, times when
someone hits a crisis that makes them grow up a
little, or not, depending on how they deal with it.
Ruth grows up a heck of a lot when she leaves
her homeland with her bitter mother-in-law.
Jonah tries but keeps backtracking. Peter has to
hit a long and winding road full of speedbumps
before he really starts to mature a little, whereas
Mary is straight off the blocks when an angel

calls her to do some fast-track growing up. And Joseph, well you can't make Prime Minister of the world's then superpower without adding a few wise wrinkles round your eyes.

But back to Ferris. There's a moment when he tells Mia that soon they will be leaving school and he will no longer see so much of his best mate Cameron. Their lives will go different ways and maybe they'll see each other once or twice, from time to time, but it won't be the same. Those days of youthful camaraderie are drawing to a close.

For the first two years of my secondary education I went to Redruth Grammar School in Cornwall. It was a relatively small place, only 600 pupils, some of the 'masters' still wore gowns. Those days were some of the best of my schooling life. By the time I had reached what we then called 'the fifth year' I just wanted to get out. By then I was at a much bigger comprehensive school in Weston-Super-Mare. No slur on that school, I just had my best days in RGS in Cornwall and never quite recovered from that school turning comprehensive in 1976 and then our family moving to Weston in 1977. In the two years in RGS I felt part of something. I never really did again. I can still remember my feelings one July evening in 1979 on the day I finished my schooling. That sense of elation that I would no longer have to go in and sit at those desks. I was and still am fairly shy and found classroom scenarios embarrassing and difficult sometimes.

In my hurry to escape school however I failed to recognise I was losing a small community of mates. Friends I had been 'forced' ☺ to spend my days with. Most of them were going on to sixth form, I went off to handle a lot of money in NatWest bank. (It was National Westminster back then – you practically got fired for abbreviating it.) It was of course another community of people, and we had some good times, usually when we should have been working... but it was an adjustment to find myself effectively losing that world of school friends (and holidays!). I was no good at staying in touch I'm afraid.

It struck me this time that Ferris Bueller's tale is partly about the end of that phase of life. Ferris takes the day to live it up. Doing some extraordinary things. A teenager's dream come true. It's a kind of glorious parting shot to being a school kid. The freedom to rebel and define your world by pushing the boundaries. When you move on all kinds of responsibilities come your way. Things that used to belong to some older people when you were at school. I did my best to stay in that rebellious attitude of mind for a while through my banking days. My first pay-check went on a 'hi fi system' and I sometimes got into trouble for enjoying myself too much in the banking world. Everything from not doing up my top button on my shirt, to claiming I was paying in money to my account from a recent bank raid. 'What the bloody hell's this?' Was the manager's cry when he found out.

Ferris's mate Cameron has a huge blow-out in the movie – rebelling against his fearful father he accidentally trashes the family Ferrari. Cameron is stunned then rustles up his best brave face.

He has rebelled, fought the system. Grown up a little. However we do not see the scene where Cameron faces his dad and the cost of what he's done. We applaud his breaking out of the unhealthy hold his old man has on him, but we're spared the possible bloodbath that might follow. Movies are like that, they can lead the viewer to some heroic battles, but avoid the messy business of having to fight them to the end.

At this point the movie *Thelma and Louise* comes to mind. Warning! Look away now if you don't want to know the end of this film...

There's a strange fairy tale finish to this rambunctious road movie. Thelma and her buddy, wishing to escape capture by the police as they flee their old lives, grip each other's hands, rev the engine, and drive straight off a cliff edge. The film conveniently freezes with the car in mid-air. Something that life doesn't do. We don't get to see the mangled wreckage when it hits the dirt below. To state the obvious – don't try that at home.

I guess tales like that of Ferris are wonderful corners of escape for us. A day in the life that we don't get to have. A coming-of-age tale with a lot of the consequences ironed out.

Indy.

Though it's now impossible for me to name a favourite film (I love too many), I do have an all-time favourite film character. The name's Jones, Indiana Jones. He somehow embodies the derring-do of Tintin (who I loved in the books) and the thrills and action of Bond. But the plots are a little easier to follow. And Indy relies on his wits rather than a tube of exploding toothpaste and a garrotting wire in his watch winder. Plus Indy trips and bumbles a lot more. And that's always endearing, a hero who might well get bruised and battered on his way to saving the world. Suave and sophisticated? Nope. I don't think so. There are also jungles and castles and trapdoors and secret tunnels in Indy's world, along with spears, poison darts, rats, snakes, creepy-crawlies, giant cobwebs and massive boulders. And for one film, James Bond is his dad! Plus – you get Harrison Ford! Who surely invented wry humour. And if not he should have done. It was Mr Ford who put the comedy into the first three *Star Wars* films. (Don't ask me which number episodes they were, it's all too complicated for me.)

But just thinking of Indiana Jones makes me smile. And my absolute favourite outing is the first one. Because of Karen Allen as Marion Ravenwood, a tough and feisty adventurer up for rivalling Indy any day. The bad guys are after the biblical Ark of the Covenant – the box containing the Ten Commandments. Get hold of that and you might just get hold of God himself. Or at least his power. A misleading notion but you know – the whole thing's a fiction. So Indy sets out with Marion to nail the bad guys and rescue the Ark.

It's said that Spielberg and Lucas concocted this film when they were lying on a beach together having conquered the world with *Star Wars* and *Jaws*. Steve tells George he's interested in making a Bond movie, but George says he has a better idea than that, and promptly tells him about a half-finished script based on the Boys Own adventures from the 1930s. And before you can say 'Snakes, why did it have to be snakes?' Harrison Ford appears with a whip and a hat and a battered leather jacket. Actually it took longer than that. But you get the picture. We all got the picture actually. It went massive.

By the time the third film came along Sir Connery had been signed up as Jones senior and they were all out there looking for the Holy Grail. The cup from the last supper. And although this is a daft idea – there were four cups in any Passover meal, and the grail itself would have no real power – I do like the scene where Indy must choose the right cup from hundreds on display. Instead of the diamond encrusted goblet chosen by the pesky ne'er-do-well baddie, Indy chooses one that is plain, an ordinary cup for a carpenter. And that I like. It seems to sum up the earthy nature of the way of Jesus. The son of God who moved into the neighbourhood, amongst the poor and the outcasts. A king like no other. No pomp or ceremony, no slaves or palaces. To paraphrase from Isaiah 53 – nothing much about him to catch our eye. Except of course for his kindness and courage and devotion to justice. A king who knew what oppression and hardship was, one with splinters in his skin and stones in his shoes. The real deal.

'You chose wisely,' the knight guarding the cups tells Indy on his plain and simple cup selection. As opposed to the ne'er-do-well who drank from his jewel-spattered antique only to find his body shrivelling up and his head disintegrating.

'He chose poorly,' the knight says. Now there's an understatement.

Pulp Fiction.

I am one of those people who immediately fell for Quentin Tarantino. I saw his first film *Reservoir Dogs* in a packed cinema in London on a Sunday evening. And most of those watching were young guys. I seem to recall looking around and thinking about that audience. Here was a bunch of young men come to see a story of guys, tension and violence. Well I knew a book full of those kind of stories. I saw *Reservoir Dogs* four times, I went twice in one day for the second and third viewings. The style seemed so fresh to me, it seemed to grab you by the lapels and refuse to let you go. Even though the film is quite talkie and the action mostly set in a single warehouse. I went home and started writing a script myself. *Without Reason.*

It was a new take on the crucifixion, set in a barn, and perpetrated by criminals in black suits. See what I did there? I didn't know a thing about writing screenplays but such was the inspiration from watching Quentin's *Dogs*. It stirred me to want to tell the gospel stories all over again. Incidentally Mr T's title means nothing really, Tarantino had worked in a video rental store and he got weary of summoning the energy to pronounce the title of the film *Au Revoir Les Enfants*. So he turned it into the stubby *Reservoir Dogs*. When Mr T's second film *Pulp Fiction* came out I went four times to see that one. I just loved the way he played with structure and time. And there were so many great characters in so many interlinking tales. Tarantino seemed to work so hard at constructing his films. The credits, the songs, the camera work, the dialogue... oh and everything else he threw in. And he was just telling made-up stories! (Though he might disagree.) And here I was, wanting to communicate a much more crucial message. (Again, he might disagree.) But seeing his films spurred me on. Be more creative, Dave! Be more unusual! Be more original, Dave. More unexpected. Draw on things not normally used to communicate the Bible. Don't be scared to try things, Dave! Years later when I saw his provocatively titled *Inglourious Basterds* I left the cinema with the same feelings. I need to work harder with the stories I tell. With the talks I give. With the presentations I prepare.

I'm a great believer in the power of entertainment. We have been given the gift of imagination for a reason. To draw the audience in, to celebrate and illustrate what is genuine and real and uplifting about life. To point out what matters, to home in on the darkness and set a light within it. I passionately believe that Jesus's stories stayed in the minds of his audience because they were good. Really good. Shocking. Funny. Startlingly good. And creatively told. He wrongfooted them, made them laugh and gasp, said tough things with a smile and an open hand. After watching *Pulp Fiction* I wrote a screenplay interlinking a few of Jesus's stories about money. Later that became a short novel, *Spondulix.*

The prophets can be dab hands with their imaginative storytelling and powerful images too. Just the other day I came across this in The Message Bible:

"The fact is that the false prophets lied to my people. They've said, 'No problem; everything's just fine,' when things are not at all fine. When people build a wall, they're right behind them slapping on whitewash. Tell those who are slapping on the whitewash, 'When a torrent of rain comes and the hailstones crash down and the hurricane sweeps in and the wall collapses, what's the good of the whitewash that you slapped on so liberally, making it look so good?' (Ezekiel 13 v 10-12)

No one's actually building a wall, and no one is hanging in the shadows with a bucket of whitewash. The whole thing is a dramatic picture, a metaphor, which is what makes it memorable. Perhaps Jesus had this in mind when he told his yarn about two housebuilders. The line about the torrent of rain and the hailstones and the hurricane, melodramatic weather or what? It's the kind of storm you might see in the Simpsons. Or the Marvel Universe. But it makes the point about how we construct our living, and to be wary of the whitewash.

The prophets can be extreme. I won't dwell on Isaiah and Micah wandering around butt naked, which they do (Micah's even howling like a wolf as he does it), but let's ponder on Jeremiah's wild donkeys for a moment. These aren't just any wild donkeys, these are donkeys on heat. Desperate for some... well... how's your father. As we used to say. Or rumpy-pumpy perhaps. I'll stop there. The point is that Jeremiah is accusing the people of being like that. Chasing after anything that brings quick satisfaction and gratification. But he doesn't say that, instead he talks about randy donkeys. This is a graphic picture. And it's memorable. A powerful jab in the ribs to make us think about what is important in life. Oh and there is a lady camel too. Desperate for a man camel. Have a look at Jeremiah 2 verses 23-25. The people have fallen for the wrong gods, the wrong priorities, and now they are smitten.

But now that I've filled your head with collapsing walls and desperate donkeys, back to Mr T. The one moment from *Pulp Fiction* that I have drawn on a few times is when two hitmen are having breakfast in a diner, discussing the way one of them, Jules, has survived being fired on at point blank range. Jules is convinced that God got involved. The bullets went all round him, tracing his frame in the wall, but nothing hit him. And in spite of his partner Vincent's protestations he remains convinced. And he is in grave danger of changing his ways. Becoming someone entirely different. He doesn't know whether you could call his experience of survival a miracle, but he knows that God was in there somewhere. Not a bad way to look at some of those strange coincidences and those unexpected, good moments. Are they miracles? Maybe. Sometimes it's hard to tell. But perhaps we can say with Jules... God got involved.

There is a preposterous and thrilling moment in Tarantino's revenge flick *Kill Bill*. The Bride, as she is known, is buried alive, left for dead. She is knocked out cold and wakes up in a box, deep in the ground. Surely this is the end of her quest. No escape now. No chance for her. But then...

the impossible happens. She begins to punch her way through the box and, inch by inch, up through the ground above. Until eventually she shoves her head through the mud and the earth, gasping for breath in an exhilarating resurrection moment. Thrilling! Extraordinary! Impossible! Outrageous! Not a bad allegorical moment then, for the genuine resurrection of Jesus, back from the tomb, fresh from death. Against all odds.

One final small thought from *Pulp Fiction*. When Bruce Willis's boxing character Butch escapes from a terrible situation, he jumps on a bike and thunders away to safety. As he goes we catch a glimpse of the name etched on the bike. Butch escapes on a thing called *Grace.*

Sing Street & Once.

I often listen to Simon Mayo and Mark Kermode's Wittertainment Film Review programme on Radio 5 Live. (Hello to Jason Isaacs.) And a few years ago I heard the good doctor Kermode wittering on about a little film called *Sing Street*. It's about a group of teenagers who form a band in Ireland in the 1980s and I knew I had to give it a watch. I wasn't disappointed. It's a perfect film about growing up, music, love, life, youth, adventure and breaking free. An early scene where young Conor first meets Raphina is one of my all-time favourites. She tells him she is a model. She isn't. He tells her he has a band and they have a song and they are making a video. He doesn't and they don't and they aren't. But it's the start of a beautiful thing. If you pushed me into the corner of your classic Regal mono-plex and threatened to beat me with your old Blockbuster Membership card then I could be pressed into saying that it's my all-time favourite film. It isn't. It just is on some days.

Later in the film Raphina jumps into the sea for the band's second video, even though she can't swim. After she has been rescued she tells Conor that she has done it for their art. 'You can never do anything by half, do you understand that?' Wholeheartedness. Something I constantly struggle with, and this moment from *Sing Street* is a great reminder. A nudge. Decades ago I had a VCR recording of a documentary called *Heart of Darkness*. It had been shot by Francis Ford Coppola's wife and was about him making *Apocalypse Now*. Part way through you discover that the great Coppola has re-mortgaged his

67

house to cover the costs of this overbudget film project. It struck me back then, that here was this artist willing to risk pretty much everything on a movie. Was I so fully committed to what I was doing?

Sing Street was directed by John Carney. It was his third film, his first being the low-budget *Once*. Others had told me I should watch this and eventually Lynn and I got round to doing so. *Once* is about a busking hoover-fixer who meets an aspiring singer. The film is almost documentary style at times as it details their time together. The heart of the story is the scene when the unnamed guy and girl get together round a piano in a music shop, to write a song from scratch. Carney managed to capture a sense of the two of them in genuine harmony as they created together.

I often go hunting for news and articles about films I've seen and I was amazed to discover that the two actors, Markéta Irglovám and Glen Hansard, had won an Oscar! Yes! I know! Who'd have thought it! This small Irish picture had found awards glory. The Oscar was for that very song, called *Falling Slowly*, created by the two actors. When they got up to collect the award Glen Hansard delivered his speech but as Markéta went to the mic the music cut in and she had to leave. In a small way it's a heart-breaking moment. HOWEVER. If you watch this clip on YouTube (look for 'Falling Slowly Oscars') you then discover something wonderful. The presenter, John Stewart, interrupts the proceedings to invite her back and to give her the opportunity to say her thank you and share a little of her story. 'Fair play to those who dare to dream,' she says, 'and don't give up.'

Perseverance is one of life's great themes. And it's all over the Bible. We may race through the book of Acts, imaging one miracle-filled day after another, but in truth years pass between the various events. Acts is like a greatest hits collection, the key moments, the vital conversions and confrontations. The first seven chapters span two years, but the next five cover fourteen. There may only be four pages between Stephen being martyred in chapter seven and Peter's miraculous prison break in chapter twelve, but in reality it's well over a decade. What were you doing fourteen years ago? That's the length of time we're talking about. There are thousands of days where the people hang on and keep doing the ordinary things. There are 400 years between the Old and New Testaments. 400! The prophet Malachi promises that change is coming (righteousness will rise like the sun and the people will leap with joy!) and then centuries pass before a young woman gives birth in the dark backstreets of Bethlehem.

This way of faith is a marathon.

Fair play to those who dream, so keep holding on to your vision of the son of righteousness, and don't give up.

Shrek.

I don't really know why but I don't get on with animated movies. Or cartoons as we used to call them. They've never floated my boat. Or hakuna-ed my matata. Not really. I get the notion that they are works of art, crafted with genius, sweat and love, but... well... I'd rather watch Robert DeNiro looking in a mirror saying, 'You talking to me?' Even the much lauded *Toy Story* didn't convert me to the church of Pixar.

And then... Andrew Adamson came along with the glorious *Shrek*. Laugh? I nearly fell off my talking donkey. I just loved that film, it sent up those Disney classics in the kind of way that made my jaw drop and my sides ache. It seemed so anarchic. Were you allowed to have Princess Fiona sing in such a way that the sweet little bird nearby exploded? From the very start, with Shrek emerging from his outside toilet in the credits, it's everything I ever wanted from an irreverent cartoon classic.

'You know what – maybe there's a good reason donkey's shouldn't talk.' So says Shrek to his prattling sidekick as they head off into the unknown together.

'Ogres are like onions,' Shrek explains to him. 'You mean they stink?' says Donkey. 'They make you cry? You leave them out in the sun and they get all brown and start sprouting little white hairs?'

It's the stuff of dialogue legend.

But you can only do that kind of thing once. *Shrek 2* just seemed to me to be playing catch up. Plus John Lithgow was hard to follow as the evil Lord Farquaad. Who else could conduct an interrogation scene with a gingerbread man like this:

Gingerbread man: 'Do you know the muffin man?'

Farquaad: 'The muffin man?'

'The muffin man.'

'Yes I know the muffin man... who lives on Drury Lane?' etc.

So clever and silly. And laugh out loud funny

I do have one or two other animated favourites. *Captain Underpants, Flushed Away* and *The Wrong Trousers*. In fact the Aardman stuff is always entertaining. (*Early Man, The Curse of the Were-Rabbit* and *Pirates! In an Adventure with Scientists!*) It's always so fabulously self-deprecating. Disney's message of 'Just believe in yourself and you can do anything' is all well and good, but no matter how hard I grit my teeth and clench my backside I'll never be President of the USA, or Prime Minister of the good ol' UK. Self-belief is useful but the ultimate message woven through the biblical adventures is that people can do it because God is with them. Moses was no Six Million Dollar Man, and Esther wasn't Wonder Woman. But God was with them. They were both well aware of their vulnerabilities. And that's what he was able to use, their reliance on him. Along with their strengths, personalities, experience, hearts, minds and wills.

The two lead rats in *Flushed Away*, Roddy and Rita, are voiced by Kate Winslet and Hugh Jackman. I instantly fell for Rita, with her cool union jack trousers and witty repartee. There was no getting one up on her. And then there's poor, hapless, likeable Roddy, out of his depth and doing his best to keep up. There is a brilliant scene where he watches Rita gracefully leap from a great height to a gentle safe landing, and follows her only to hit half a dozen hard objects on the way down. Including the head of a hammer in his hoojamaflips. And then when Roddy lands and straightens up he is belted in the same region by a flying football. Poor guy. That clip reminds me so much of poor Peter, playing catch up all the time with Jesus. Tripping over his feet and slamming into hammerheads and footballs as he tries to appear in control.

I once wrote a monologue in which Peter recounted his greatest achievements. He began all puffed up with pride, but as he read account after account of banana skin moments, so he became more and more deflated. Poor Peter. Such good news for the rest of us. I'm forever tripping over my own ego, and slamming into hammerheads as I fall from the great height of my own overblown view of myself. Thankfully we're all playing catch up when it comes to God, and thankfully he slows down so he can walk with us and pick us up. Time after time after time.

Jojo Rabbit.

Occasionally a film comes along that is so loaded with satire it split's the audience. Taika Waititi's 2019 movie about a little boy with an invisible friend did just that. It is set in Germany towards the end of World War Two, and tells the tale of Jojo, a little boy in the Hitler Youth. The problem here is that his invisible friend is called Adolf. He has a little black moustache and looks uncannily like an infamous Nazi. Jojo's invisible friend is Mr Hitler. Jojo is trying to be a good member of the Hitler Youth but the others take the mickey and before long he is injured out. Then he discovers a young Jewish girl hiding in a secret place beyond his sister's bedroom wall. His mother is clearly not telling him everything.

Google's dictionary defines satire as – the use of humour, irony, exaggeration, or ridicule to expose and criticise people's stupidity or vices, particularly in the context of contemporary politics and other topical issues. I'd say that sums up this film. Hitler comes out of it looking ridiculous and callous, and eventually Jojo has the good sense to boot him through a window. Jojo's initial racist views are lambasted, not least by the courageous, wise and vulnerable Elsa. The girl in the wall. She lampoons his strange and monstrous ideas about Jews, showing him just how ridiculous his ideas are. Ultimately Jojo begins to see clearly, and discover the truth about humanity. However, the problem with satire is, taken at face value, it can be misunderstood.

When Gordon Gecko announced that 'Greed is good!' in Oliver Stone's *Wall Street*, the yuppies stood up and applauded. What a great idea. The film portrayed how bad this idea was, but Gecko's speech got taken out of context. When Jesus said, 'Tear down this temple and in three days I'll rebuild it!' he wasn't necessarily being satirical, but he was being creative with his words. And he got misunderstood. His enemies twisted his message and accused him of threats against their beloved stone monument. He was in fact predicting the destruction they would bring on him, and the temple of his own body. But they couldn't see that.

I recently read a satirical piece on Twitter about how it was perfectly fine for folk to not wear face masks in the pandemic. 'Just,' the writer said, 'as it was fine for those who work in his restaurant to not wash their hands after a trip to the bathroom, and to handle the food on the customer's plate. After all, most people recover from food poisoning. What's the problem? It's fine.' I had to read this piece twice because at first I missed the point and wondered why on earth anyone would gladly support the idea of not wearing face masks. But it's not that. It's the opposite. And it's memorable as a result. The thing has stuck in my mind.

Satire can be powerful. And vulnerable.

To change tack for a moment, and move on from satire to the unexpected ways that something bad can be used for good (e.g. the way that this tale about Jojo's indoctrination highlights how misguided these ideas actually are.) I recently came across a documentary film on YouTube entitled *China's Schindlers*. (That's the thing about films these days, the term is more fluid and the available channels more diverse.) The reference here is to German businessman Oskar Schindler but the documentary told the stories of German businessman John Rabe and Chinese diplomat Dr Feng Shan Ho.

In December 1937, the Japanese army entered the Chinese capital Nanking. And so the horrors started, as the invading army began killing, torturing and raping the occupants. John Rabe worked for Siemens in Nanking, he was also a member of the Nazi party, believing that Hitler had put Germany on its feet, but was unaware of the oppressive nature of the party. As the Japanese army approached the city most of the foreign workers fled, only 22 stayed. When the massacres began Rabe and the others set up the Nanking Safety Zone, a place where refugees fleeing the slaughter could find protection. The Japanese government had agreed not to attack parts of the city that did not contain Chinese military forces. So Rabe and the others persuaded the Chinese soldiers to leave the safe zone to make it safe for civilians. It is estimated that around 250,000 Chinese were killed in the six week massacre, but it's also estimated that Rabe and his friends saved a similar number of lives. Somewhere between 200,000 and 250,000 people. One of the extraordinary things is that, when Japanese forces attempted to invade the safe zone Rabe would approach them with something in his hand – he held up his Swastika armband. And the Japanese, in a pact with the Nazi party, would retreat. Likewise, when the city was bombed Rabe covered a bomb-shelter containing Chinese citizens with his Nazi flag. This kept the planes from attacking it. He and the other humanitarians would sometimes walk the streets at night, doing their best to intervene in attacks. He also carefully documented what was going on. But how extraordinary, and unexpected, that a swastika, a symbol which represents so much evil and horror, in this one instance could be used to protect people and save lives. After the war he and his family fell into terrible poverty back in Germany, and when news of this travelled back to China, the people sent money and brought food for Rabe and his family.

Meanwhile in Vienna, Chinese diplomat Dr Feng Shan Ho was also saving lives. In 1938, after Kristallnacht, the night of broken glass, life became much more difficult for the Jews in Austria. If they could get visas they could leave, but most other countries were closing their doors. However, China was still open. It was quite possible for Austrian Jews to travel to Shanghai and start a new life there in freedom. All they needed was a visa. And what did Dr Ho have in spades? Visas. He began issuing as many as he could, helping families to escape the country. Putting his career and his life on the line to help others who were being persecuted. When the consulate closed and he was forced out, he rented a small apartment and didn't stop. He continued issuing visas for the Jewish families. No one knows how many lives he saved, but it is likely to be in the thousands.

Two very different men, bringing light and hope into deepest darkness.

I dearly believe that God can use all kinds of unexpected people, tools, events and objects, to bring his compassion to those who need it. God is bigger than our ideas about him. I heard that saying years ago, and it must be true. Because we all have limited vision, or as St Paul put it, we see God through a smudgy window, or a glass darkly. Who would have thought that crucifixion, that appalling means of execution, could become the channel for the salvation of the cosmos? Or that St Paul, initially one of the biggest haters of Christianity, would write – 'Wherever we may go, there is nothing that can ever separate us from the love of God revealed in Jesus his son.' That's one of the reasons we need each other, because you can show me something of God's grace that I have not seen for myself.

Papillon.

I first saw *Papillon* in my early teens, in the 1970s. It starred Steve McQueen, who I had seen and loved in *The Great Escape*. The Cooler King with the even cooler attitude. *Papillon* was another escape movie, but this one had a darker heart. In 1933 Henri Charrière, a.k.a. Papillon (butterfly) was shipped to the French penal colony in humid and brutal French Guiana. On the way he befriended Louis Dega (Dustin Hoffman), a forger with money to spare. In the years that follow Papillon does his level best to say bye bye to the harsh and fetid prison. He fails more often than he succeeds. And a motorbike won't get him over the hills and far away in this yarn. I recently watched the new version, with Charlie Hunnam in Mr McQ's role. It's good but... you just don't feel that heat, or sense the sweat and putrid air in the same way somehow.

I read Charriere's book in 1988, and it dropped a little seed into my thinking. The book is longer and features many more adventures, but when Papillon is floating to freedom on a coconut raft, smack in the middle of an endless sea, he looks up at the sky and around at the water and starts talking about God. And how nature speaks of his presence. I almost did a double take. Here, in this brutal, squalid book about prison and the battles to break out, was this moment which brought the focus right back on God. I wasn't reading a Christian book, not at all, and yet God was waiting for me on this page. And that stayed with me, the idea that you can encounter God anywhere, and not least in ordinary books and films.

In the book *Touching the Void*, which is also a film, Joe Simpson tells an extraordinary story of surviving a fall while mountain climbing in the Peruvian Andes. In the book, at the point when he wanted to give up, he describes hearing a voice in his head telling him to stay awake and keep going. He writes about remembering that his mum used to pray for him and wondered if she was doing so at that point. I couldn't help wondering whether the two were connected. That the voice in his head was God's urging him to stay alive and not give up. Jesus spoke of the signs of the kingdom of God at large in the world. And I can't help thinking that they are everywhere, often anonymous and subtle, but there for us to spot and ponder their meaning. I wonder if God waits for us all over the place.

Yesterday.

Occasionally a film comes along that instantly scoops me up, and I do my best to watch it several times. It happened with *Reservoir Dogs, Pulp Fiction, JFK, Goldeneye, Notting Hill, What We Did on Our Holiday* and *Spotlight.*

And *Yesterday.*

Richard Curtis's wonderful film about a world where no one but Jack Malik knows the songs of the Beatles. The posters actually advertised the premise incorrectly. They announced that everyone else had forgotten the Beatles, but as the story unfolds it's almost as if they never existed. And this is rather fortunate for Jack because he is a failing singer-songwriter on the verge of giving up. He doesn't have enough decent songs and just can't get a break, until the night a strange accident puts him in hospital, where he wakes up to find that the Beatles as he knows them, never existed. And so he begins scribbling down their songs and recording a few of them. Before he knows it, Ed Sheeran is knocking on his door (yes, the real Ed Sheeran) and fame is a-calling.

Imagine if you were part of a crowd gathered around a painting of twelve men eating together. People are oohing and aahing about it. There is no food on the table and a gap in the middle of the group, but no one seems to notice that. They just thinking the picture is fabulous. What you want to do though is grab a chair, leap on it and yell, 'Hang on! There's something missing from this picture!' Three things in fact. Bread, wine and Jesus. You see, Jack Malik lives in a world where no one knows about the Beatles. We live in a world where it sometimes feels as if a lot of folk don't know about the carpenter from Nazareth. As if he'd never been. As if Leonardo DiCaprio… oh sorry… I mean da Vinci, had never painted a picture of the last supper. Or if he did all the best bits were missing. It's become just a bunch of mates arguing round an empty table. The heart of it, the reality, the life… is missing.

Jack Malik appropriates the Beatles back catalogue, starts singing those great songs. Admittedly at first he does it for gain and fame. But he's getting the music out there. And people want to join in. There is a great clip on YouTube of a huge crowd in Trafalgar Square singing along to *Hey Jude*, it doesn't matter whether they can sing or not, they are all invited to join in. Search on YouTube for 'Hey Jude flash mob' and you should find it. It's a T-Mobile advert.

I love it because everyone is welcome. Some can sing, some can't. And that's the invitation from Jesus, make a start, join in, it doesn't matter if you are any good at being a Christian, just take a step. He's not looking for experts, he's never really had any to work with anyway. He wants real people, ordinary, bumbling, hungry people. Those willing to find out what's truly going on at the Last Supper.

The Great Escape.

Steve McQueen is allowed to take his baseball and glove into solitary confinement. I'd never thought about it before. I just loved the sight of him bouncing that ball off the walls and catching it in that huge, padded glove. But... really? In solitary? Isn't it supposed to be a punishing experience? I don't think they'd let you take your smart phone and charger in there. And there's also the question of his outfit. Everyone else has been captured in their dusty old uniforms. Not Steve. He gets to wear jeans, boots and a cool t-shirt. Again, I never minded really, I aspired to that kind of outfit as a kid. But thinking about it now...

There's so much to love about this film. The fantastic British cast. Plus Mr McQ and the great Jim Rockford, a.k.a. James Garner. Also very cool. I love the scene where Big X (Richard Attenborough) tells McQueen about the planned escape. When Big X tells him how many are going McQueen's reaction is priceless, 'Two hundred and fifty!?!!' he exclaims. 'You're crazy. You oughta be locked up. Two hundred and fifty guys just walkin' down the road, just like that?' And then there's the doomed motorbike chase. Every time I see it I think he might just make it this time. But no. Apparently McQueen (who loved bikes and cars) doubled as a German in filming the chase, so at one point he is actually chasing himself. Perhaps he'd have got away if he'd left them to it.

I've seen it many times but still get a thrill when I start watching it all over again. The tragic tale of the real story is that it resulted in the Germans clamping down on further escapes. So it became much more dangerous to break out. Seventy-six of the Great Escapers got out of the camp. Only three made it to freedom. It was a costly venture.

And then there are the 50 men who were brought back and shot. In the film they are gathered together in a field and a machine gun opens fire from the back of a truck, but in reality they were taken off in ones and twos, and dispatched with a pistol. After the war the RAF took up the cause and scoured the country, tracking down those who had murdered the unarmed escapers. In the film *A Bridge Too Far*, there is a scene where five of the allied officers are gathered together to reflect on the battle. When each man comes up with a different reason as to why things went so wrong, the Polish officer Major General Sosabowski replies, 'Doesn't matter what it was... when one man says to another, "I know what to do today, let's play a war game..." everybody dies.'

A Bridge Too Far is another film I could watch again and again. But more on that later.

The Dam Busters.

I revisited this film several times when visiting my dad in his later years in a care home. He loved it as I did and so it was a frequent choice when we were together. Re-watching it I found the character of Barnes Wallis inspiring, an inventor who had to battle the odds and stick with his vision of the bouncing bomb. Time and again the trials failed, but that didn't deter him. He thought differently, stayed the course and went on believing. I find stories of folk battling uphill to change things inspiring. But it's an honest film too. And we see Wallis's disturbed reaction at the end when he learns how many pilots have been killed in the bombing raid. There is no victory lap. Wallis is aware of the cost. Guy Gibson, the pilot who headed up the mission, was probably the first clean cut hero to inspire me. He was played by Richard Todd, who had been a real-life hero in the D-Day Landings on the 6th June 1944. So that added to the appeal. He seemed good-natured, yet courageous and dedicated, with a firm grasp of the mission. You feel the burden of loss through his character too as the story closes out.

Went the Day Well is another war film which tries to capture both the heroism and the cost of the conflict. Made during the war it tells of a village secretly invaded by a bunch of German soldiers disguised as British troops. There's a shocking scene where the postmistress is clubbed to death before she can spread the news of the soldiers' real identity. This is one of the things I love about stories. You can tell gritty true tales, and say difficult things, and rather than shoving these at people you offer them with an open hand.

Jesus was a pass master at this. He is surrounded by an antagonistic audience of religious 'experts' when he tells his story about a lost sheep. Instead of challenging them, and telling them even they are lost, he tells everyone about the big party thrown in heaven for those who come back to God. 'There is more rejoicing in heaven over the one repentant sinner than over the 99 who don't need to,' he says. Now, we all need to repent, no matter how knowledgeable we are with our theology. But rather than banging his head against the wall of their short-sightedness, Jesus suggests the 'experts' might just be missing out. Terrible sinner repenting? Yay! Big knees up, massive party, food, drink and laughter. 'Expert' who doesn't need to repent? Er... tumbleweed. Cobwebs. Dust and shadows. So... d'you want a big party? Or are you happy to miss out? Jesus uses his story to open a conversation, rather than shut one down. A group of us guys at Lee Abbey gathered in our house once to watch the film *In Bruges*. It's an earthy, brutal, sweary film, and yet it opened up the conversation, afterwards we chatted for quite a while about a whole shedload of things.

In Bruges.

And on the subject of *In Bruges*, it's a great example of the way a story can be about very bad people, and dark circumstances, yet also speak to us about truth and light. Ray and Ken are hitmen hiding out in the Belgian city of Bruges. Ken loves it but Ray is bored and he drives Ken mad. And yet, as circumstances buckle and twist and take a turn for the very worst, Ken wants the best for Ray. He believes in him and is willing to lay everything on the line for him. It reminds me that you don't have to tell 'nice' stories to spark conversations about good things.

Jesus knew that well. His stories feature bad people. Like the judge who cares not one jot for justice and who would rather see a woman starve just so he can be left in peace. Or a bunch of tenants who turn into dangerous predators and start dishing out violence on anyone who tries to turn them off the land. Or the older brother who won't go searching for his lost sibling, hoping that some harm might come to him. Or the rich idiot who refuses to share what he has to help those around him. He'd rather stuff his possessions into groaning barns, while others suffer. These stories were told to help us engage with the ways of God's kingdom. To wrestle with reality. They are intended to shock us, to wake us up. They are not nice stories. The problem for some of us now is that we see them as 'Bible stories' and as nice, holy, perfect tales, and that can sometimes diffuse the shock. Remove the sting that makes them confrontational and memorable. We're supposed to say, 'Eh?! What!!' And not just – 'This is the word of the Lord.'

A Bridge Too Far.

An absolute epic. One of those films I watch and wonder how Richard Attenborough ever managed to make it. So many massive scenes. So many actors. So many bridges. A war film to top them all. One of those tales too that you always hope might end a little happier, a little bit more *all right* the next time you watch it. I get that feeling with *Day of the Jackal* too. Maybe this time Edward Fox'll manage it. Even though he is a baddie. The fantastic Mr Fox is of course in *A Bridge Too Far* along with Sean Connery, Robert Redford, Dirk Bogarde, Elliot Gould, Michael Caine, Gene Hackman, Laurence Olivier, Liv Ullman, James Caan, Ryan O'Neil, Hardy Kruger, Maximilian Schell, Anthony Hopkins and a cast of thousands more. All accompanied by a brilliant, rousing soundtrack.

To this day I have still never quite grasped the actual journey the mission is taking, involving four bridges and the Rhine river. I do know it takes way longer than expected and the scenes at the last bridge at Arnhem become increasingly desperate and heart-breaking, as Anthony Hopkins and his men do their level best to hold on. I was once told that those who fought desperately to free the town are still remembered there to this day. The contrast is appallingly stark between the scenes of joy and celebration as Hopkins and his men first drive into Arnhem, and then the desolation a few days later after the town has been pummelled by tanks and gunfire. I have used these scenes to talk of Jesus's warnings about Jerusalem. The jubilant streets as he rides in on Palm Sunday, and his predictions about what will happen to the city if the people persist in attempts at uprising. A prophecy fulfilled 40 years later when the Romans piled in and levelled the place. Who knows how many might have turned to Jesus then, realising that his words were true. 'You do not realise what makes for peace,' he says, his heart breaking for the people of this precious place. Jesus is very much a peaceful hero. Not a conquering one. Not easy to get our heads round that.

We are so used to tales of violent victories. George slays the dragon, Jack hacks down the beanstalk, the crusaders ride off in armour to take back the Holy city, Maximus Decimus Meridius battles Commodus in the Roman arena, the man with no name infiltrates the gang of desperados and shoots them all up. That's what is so remarkable about films like *Gandhi, Schindler's List* and *Hotel Rwanda*. Paul Rusesabagina was manager of the Hôtel des Mille Collines in Kigali when the Rwandan genocide broke in 1994. He ended up saving the lives of 1268 Hutus and Tutsis by giving them refuge in the luxury hotel. In his book he tells of the way the militia would turn up heavily armed and blood-spattered, demanding access to those he was sheltering. Paul would sit them down in his office, ply them with drinks and engage them in pleasant conversation, always looking to tap into the humanity buried somewhere within those killers. Every time he managed to send them away having avoided any slaughter. He believed that it was possible to find good within everyone and that view somehow drew it out of others time and again. Like Oskar Schindler he fought against tyranny with the weapons of peace. In his book, *An Ordinary Man*, he wrote about the way villagers at odds with one another used to sit down and drink tea, it was hard he said, to stay at loggerheads when you were eating and drinking together. Perhaps that is another facet of the offer of bread and wine from Jesus. Breaking bread together feeds and changes us as a community, not merely as individuals.

In Richard Attenborough's *Gandhi* there is a pertinent scene when the people march on the Dharasana salt works, in a peaceful protest over salt tax. As the soldiers beat down the unarmed protesters it is these armed guards that reveal their ugly side. They only have sticks and guns, the people have a vision and the hunger for positive change. And that's costly. As we find with Jesus. Offer your enemy the other cheek and they might well slap it hard, live your life with open hands rather than fists and sooner or later someone will stick nails through your palms. 'I want you to be known by the love you show each other,' Jesus tells his disciples, in the BBC mini-series *The Passion*. A road less travelled. Especially in movie-land.

To end with a jarring gear change, one of the few non-violent illustrations of atonement in film occurs in the comedy *Groundhog Day*. When stranded TV presenter Phil puts himself up for sale in a charity auction, Rita, the love of his life, pays a hefty price to get him. She's willing to pay handsomely for his life. A friend Luke mentioned this scene to me. Luke works for the Bible Society and heads up an annual competition *The*

Pitch, inviting filmmakers to submit ideas for original short films which bring the Bible off the page. In a way, that beautifully sums up what films do for me. They bring the Bible off the page, demonstrate the way that the timeless, ever-relevant biblical themes, principles and stories are at work (or not) in people's lives. They help flesh out the stories too. There are no walk-on parts in the Bible, no two-dimensional characters. They all have personalities, and foibles, and mood-swings and back stories. Like you and me.

Whistle Down the Wind.

I don't know if this was the first film I ever saw at the cinema, but I often say it is. It's certainly the first film I saw and loved. I was swept up in this tale of a bunch of youngsters who find a crook (played by Alan Bates) on the run and hiding in their barn. The kids then mistake him for Jesus. They keep him hidden and bring him food, comics and one of the kittens they have rescued. The bad guy meanwhile is bemused by all this, but makes the most of their care and attention. Jesus spoke highly of little children, bigging up their innocence and humility, and that certainly comes across here. Plus I fell for Hayley Mills. Of course I did.

I didn't realise it at the time but I was having my first experience of a gospel retold. Ok, in this case the crook really is a crook, but there was something wonderfully allegorical about a man loved by the ordinary kids yet hunted by the grim authorities who, as far as those kids are concerned, lack real understanding. When the guy in the barn is arrested the children watch from a distance as he stands there, arms stretched out in a crucifixion pose.

Some time after seeing this we went to a showing of the film *Kidnapped*. I was bitterly disappointed. It wasn't anything like *Whistle Down the Wind*. And there was no Hayley Mills. I had been spoilt. The first film I had seen was an absolute classic, but I was discovering that not all films are like that. I've had that deflated feeling many times since. Sometimes because a film has not been all I wanted it to be. That said, some of these underwhelming films have then grown on me over time. I guess you have to allow a film to be what it's not. If that makes sense.

I almost felt like giving up on cinema altogether when we went to see *Four Weddings and a Funeral.* I had heard so much and it was supposed to be funnier than... oooh... the funniest film you've ever seen. But it didn't make me laugh. And I was bitterly annoyed about that! As the years have passed, and I have enjoyed other Richard Curtis films, I'll admit I have softened towards it. And at the time we did take inspiration from the title when we sent out cards for our wedding, inviting people to *One Wedding and a Reception.*

One of my favourite moments in *Whistle Down the Wind* occurs when the children ask the vicar why one of their kittens died. The little boy Charles gave it to 'Jesus' in the barn to look after. The vicar waffles and mutters a few things which don't really hit the spot, and as the children walk away Charles says, in his broad Lancashire accent, 'He didn't know did he.' Sometimes we just have no idea what's going on. Or why. And to say that out loud, rather than making excuses, can be the truth that in some way sets us free.

The Last Temptation.

I'll be honest here. I get bored in church. In the worst days of my rebellion about this I used to sometimes slip out part way through a service. And one Palm Sunday I nipped home (we were living in the community at Lee Abbey at the time, so home was only a few hundred steps away) and put on *The Last Temptation*. The Palm Sunday scene in this film has a real sense of threat about it. A city full of people, some waving sticks as well as branches, all hoping that this day will turn violent. It surprised me. Unnerved me at first perhaps. But to be honest it is nearer the truth than our tradition of handing out small palm crosses.

I understand the meaning of that tradition, and the powerful symbolism of it, but when I see young boys in church having sword fights with their palm crosses, I can't help thinking that this is closer to the reality of that first day. The people were desperate for freedom and wanted an uprising. Zechariah the prophet had predicted that the new and right king would come in riding on a donkey. So yay! Bring it on. Let's kick out these Romans and that pesky double-dealer Herod. Let Jesus be the new king and let's join his army. The kingdom of God is coming. We can be great and powerful again. That's what they thought. That's why the Pharisees got all jumpy and told Jesus to tell everyone to shut up. They didn't want the Romans piling in and doing what they did best. Crucifying people.

It was refreshing and challenging to watch the scene played out in Martin Scorsese's film. And I do think at times it's good to have our preconceptions about biblical stories challenged. We cannot help but view them with our 21st century perception. Palm Sunday came alive in a whole new way. It strikes me now that we might sometimes revisit and re-enact the part of the account where Jesus rides into Jerusalem to cheering crowds, but we don't tend to re-enact him turning over the tables of the corrupt institution. Upsetting and unsettling expectations and the status quo.

In the modern retelling *Jesus of Montreal*, the table-turning scene is portrayed powerfully. The film is about a group of actors putting on a passion play, but their lives begin to reflect the biblical story. The actor playing Jesus, Daniel, visits a casting call, where the actress playing Mary Magdalene is up for a part. However, the executives and filmmakers want her to remove her top and put herself on show. Daniel is having none of this and grabbing a trestle table containing some of their equipment, he flips it over. Then he yanks cables from the back of a camera and sends the kit flying. Those in charge back away as Daniel lets his righteous anger loose and upends the predatorial situation. It's powerful because we see the sparks flying and hear the crashes as the expensive equipment is damaged. Daniel is doing real harm here. But then the system is corrupt. It's an allegorical take on the tables in the temple.

In another scene, a businessman tries to tempt Daniel away from playing the role of Jesus by taking him up to the top floor of a skyscraper, showing him the city, and talking about other more lucrative roles he might play instead. Again, Daniel is having none of it. This film cleverly digs beneath the surface for a modern audience. One of the actors in the passion play comes from a background of acting in porn films. These are characters we wouldn't normally think of as holy. Just as the fishermen and tax collectors and poor widows and fallen women were not understood to be holy. Just as the pagan Roman officer who has his eyes opened at the crucifixion would not be seen as holy. This life-giving kingdom is available to all. It's anarchic. It's spiritual punk rock. Coming from the ground up. Bypassing the systems of the day and growing up like overlooked mustard seeds – the weeds of Jesus's day.

When Scorsese's film first came out we were all supposed to be up in arms about it. Years later I discovered that he had originally wanted to make a modern gospel, but then heard about the making of *Jesus of Montreal* so instead switched to this project, which draws on the book *The Last Temptation of Christ*. That last temptation is for Jesus to come down from the cross and live a normal life, give up on his mission and walk away from giving himself for the cosmos. A temptation which he surely faced, not only as the crowd jeered at him to prove himself and leap Superman-like off those nails, but also in the garden of Gethsemane the night before, and three years previously in the wilderness we now think of as Lent. Jesus faced every temptation, we are told in Hebrews 13, so he knows what we go through, but he stayed right on course for us.

About a Boy.

Will wants to be alone. Or at least left alone. Wealthy enough to live a life of leisure he wonders how people find the time to work. Pampering, pleasure, and pastimes seem to consume all the hours available to him. *No man is an island...* so the poem goes. Well Will is, he's the exception that proves the rule. So there. Then young Marcus crashes into his life, and Marcus doesn't have the same agenda as Will. He needs a friend. Or at least a place to hide from his enemies. So one day he rings Will's bell and runs inside. And thus begins the tale about, not just one boy, but two.

There are times when I wouldn't mind being Will. Having everything on tap, with no pressures or people to please. But life doesn't work like that. Other people are both the best and worst things about our time on earth. Often in the same day. It doesn't surprise me that we're so keen to go to the moon. Or Mars. Or Pluto. Anything to escape from some of these folks down here.

As I have grown older (Me? Older? Surely not!) I realise I am becoming more introverted. I'm quite happy to sit here hitting keys and messaging from a distance. In some ways I have reverted back to my earlier years as a boy when I used to spend lots of time in my room, listening to Radio One, reading comics and books, making models and painting Airfix soldiers, and attempting to write. The world can seem a large and frightening place. In my 20s I spent seven weeks in South Africa, some of it travelling alone. When I flew to

Cambodia nine years later I was a lot less confident.

I wish I were an action man, a swashbuckler, but I'm not. Not anymore. Now I'm a teller of tales, hopefully the kind that help people through the day. The kind that are laced with faith, hope and love. When I told one of my mum's friends that I wanted to be a writer, he told me to do two things. Read other people's books and travel. Well, thanks to others I have done some travelling, but now it's down to the reading. At least with the internet I can do a certain kind of global exploring. I'm a kind of passivist really, not so much an activist, just someone who hopes that I can make a difference from my swivel chair.

Towards the end of *About a Boy* Will breaks out of his cool comfort zone to rescue Marcus. Suddenly he is no longer an island. His defences have been breached by this chaotic bundle of a boy trying to do his best for his broken-hearted mum. Marcus endeavours to sing in front of the whole school for her, but Will knows that sort of thing is social suicide. Perhaps that's why Will refrains from too much engagement with others. It's messy. But Marcus is out there, putting himself on the line, and the other kids are slow handclapping. The end is nigh. Until Will grabs a guitar and struts on stage. Suddenly Marcus is not alone, this island has come floating by, and now Will looks a bit daft too. It's something Jesus never feared. He was no island. And constantly got bashed about because of it. He still knows countless lost souls and keeps on sending folks like Will to help them, and us, out.

Brooklyn.

I was surprised to discover that the screenplay for this film was written by Nick Hornby. I love Hornby's books but he originally emerged as a writer of laddie, blokey stuff. *Fever Pitch, High Fidelity, About a Boy.* This story is one of fabulous romance and tenderness. Eilis leaves Ireland to find work and a new life in Brooklyn. At first she is terribly homesick and struggles to find a smile. Then she meets Tony, and everything changes. There is a great moment on a bus when he asks her on a date to see a movie with him. Thinking carefully, the cautious and reasonable Eilis says that she will go on two dates with him, if the first movie is a disaster, she'll give him a second chance.

Julie Walters is at her finest as Mrs Keogh, the landlady who runs the house for single girls where Eilis makes a home. She is wonderfully Irish and full of quirky guidance for the girls. When they talk too much about frivolous things at the dinner table she says, 'I'll tell you this much: I am going to ask Father Flood to preach a sermon on the dangers of giddiness. I now see that giddiness is the eighth deadly sin. A giddy girl is every bit as evil as a slothful man, and the noise she makes is a lot worse. Now, enough.'

Tony and Eilis are nervous and shy, they are not used to such romance. Though they both long for it. Their relationship reminded me of our hesitancy towards the love of God. It's often easier to serve, to obey the rules, to take on responsibility. But opening our battered hearts to God's love. That feels risky. We need help.

Little Women.

There was a period in my life when I would not have spoken too loudly about loving this film. I was into blokey stuff – I was trying to be anyway. *Gladiator, Pulp Fiction, Trainspotting,* those movies were just fine. They were what I should be watching. Nothing too tender or gentle. But then I began to realise something. I had started leading men's workshops at Lee Abbey, and after one a good friend pointed out to me that I'm not that blokey. Because I'm not. I love retelling the Bible in earthy, gritty, shocking ways, ways that often work for many guys, but that's about it. Blokeland ends there for me. It took me a while to learn this.

I seem to have been through various phases in my Christian work, a lot of them beginning with M. For nine years I was a fulltime mime artist. Then I wrote *The Bloke's Bible* and started doing 'Men's Events'. And then it was all about movies. However, I'm not a film critic, or a film buff really. I just love the Bible and want to find as many unusual ways as possible to help folk connect with it. Now. Discarding any language or protocol or traditions that get in the way. So films, television programmes, internet material, comedy clips, news stories. Anything is usable. Even stuff that seems a million miles away from Christianity.

But back to Meg, Jo, Beth and Amy. Those *Little Women.* Gretta Gerwig directed a new version in 2019, one I'm still getting used to, but this tale from 1994 is the one I love. With Winona Ryder, Susan Sarandon and Clare

Danes. I particularly love the scenes in the attic, where the four girls make up stories and act them out. And those moments where you see Jo perched at her desk, writing by candlelight, her fingers all inky as she scribbles down her latest yarn for her sisters. It's a film which tugs at my heart and lubricates my eyeballs at various times. The youthful, heady days don't hang around long enough, the March women must grow up and embrace their own lives. I wish they could stay as a family unit, wish those creative times in the attic could live on forever. But time moves on. It's unstoppable. King Canute proved it. So here's a wee reading.

Our Times

Our times are in your hands,

Our days, our nights,

The fleeting moments and long days,

The times of waiting and the times we savour.

Our times are in your hands,

The times of this planet,

Of our own small worlds,

As they turn and meander,

As we rush and stumble,

As we do our best to cling on,

Our times are in your hands.

Though we may be full of questions,

Weighed down with fears,

Muddled by reality,

We wait, we look to you.

We need you so much,

Lift our heads when the going is tough,

Warm us with your presence,

Smile on us please.

We throw our lot in with you today,

We want to want your ways,

And long for more than we have within ourselves,

So our times are in your hands,

Our ways, our steps,

Our reactions and conversations,

Our whole being, our existence,

Every moment is found in you.

Psalm 31 v 14-16

Shawshank Redemption & The GBU.

Nowadays this film tops many of those favourite film lists. In fact, as I type this today, these are the top ten films on IMDB, as voted for by those who use the site:

1. The Shawshank Redemption (1994)

2. The Godfather (1972)

3. The Godfather: Part II (1974)

4. The Dark Knight (2008)

5. 12 Angry Men (1957)

6. Schindler's List (1993)

7. The Lord of the Rings: The Return of the King (2003)

8. Pulp Fiction (1994)

9. The Good, the Bad and the Ugly (1966)

10. The Lord of the Rings: The Fellowship of the Ring (2001)

Discuss. As they say.

On *The Good, the Bad and the Ugly*, I recall watching the start of this in a packed film club at school one lunch time. This was around the advent of video players, and one of the teachers had recorded it off TV. The medium was so new that no one realised it was illegal to record a film and show it in a film club. Perhaps it wasn't even illegal at that point. Anyway, I only watched the first twenty minutes or so because I really wanted to watch it all, but had not been allowed to at home, and when my friend asked me if I'd seen it, I didn't dare admit I had not been allowed to stay up late. Instead I told him I'd missed the start of it. (Rather than most of the rest of it!) And so, I went along to watch the start all over again, probably in the hope that I'd catch a bit more than I had at home. My friend however was keen not to watch it all over again. So when we soon slipped away I'd seen the start, and nothing but the start, twice. No idea when I finally caught the rest of it. Ho hum. The trials of boyhood. I had a poster of Clint on my wardrobe door in my bedroom. I think I got it out of that hip and happening magazine, *The Radio Times*. Clint seemed to embody a mysterious and dangerous kind of hero. After all, he was the man with no name.

Why do people love *Shawshank*? Who knows, there are probably lots of reasons. It's certainly a film shot through with hope in the most difficult of situations. Andy Dufresne never gives up and he brings that life-enhancing belief to others. Whether it's more books for the library, beers on a baking hot day, or music in the prison yard. In one significant storyline the prison fixer and world-weary Red, played by Morgan Freeman, tells Andy that he used to play the harmonica but cannot see a use for it in prison. He thinks hope is a dangerous thing that can drive you mad, when all you can see are walls. So Andy lays out good money and buys Red a new harmonica, a physical symbol, a reminder, to never give up on hope. Hope is like currency to Andy, it's a sustaining thing, it energises and revives him.

I think physical reminders are powerful. You can hold them in your hand and be reminded. Remember again that nugget of truth you have been given. A couple of times I have handed out small Jenga blocks with text on the side to remind folk they are part of the temple God is building, not actually made of Jenga blocks or hunks of stone, but made of flesh and blood and bone. A temple made of people. Made of us. The text on the block reads:

For you are God's creation, precious and vital, part of God's big picture in the world, called to follow him and share his love. Ephesians 2 v 10

We are God's house. All different shaped bricks. Just yesterday I was reading about David's desire to build God a temple (in a book entitled *Men Behaving Badly*). The problem with that, author John Goldingay says, is that we want to give God a home so we can look after him, control him perhaps, whereas life is about God looking after us, giving us a home. We want to hem God in, and yet he will constantly break out of the boxes we put him in. We want to pin him down, get hold of him, whereas he wants to be roaming free, in the health clubs, sports clubs and night clubs; in the side streets, slums and back alleys; in the bars and the brothels; in the superstores and cinemas. (Especially in the cinemas ☺)

A Few Favourite One Liners.

'We've gone on holiday by mistake!'

Withnail tells a local farmer their troubles.

Withnail & I

'I don't remember it being this orange.'

Lucy, on the colour of her childhood memories.

While You Were Sleeping

'Life is full of interruptions and complications.'

Karl to Sarah when her phone keeps ringing.

Love Actually

'You see what I'm saying? What are you prepared to do?'

Malone to Elliot Ness about catching Al Capone.

The Untouchables

'You can be too old for a lot of things, you're never too old to be afraid.'

Old man Marley to Kevin in church.

'It doesn't matter how mad I was, I'd talk to my dad.'

Kevin to old man Marley in church.

Both from Home Alone

'We will never send you away.'

Jim Braddock to his son Jay.

Cinderella Man

'Find your own voice...'

'Todd thinks everything inside of him is worthless...'

'Two roads diverged in a wood and I, I took the one less travelled by and that has made all the difference.'

Mr Keating to his class.

Dead Poets Society

'You see that? Character. And for what? Nine bucks. That's just so disappointing.'

The angel posing as a shopkeeper as a customer leaves without being honest.

Family Man

'What we do in life echoes in eternity.'

Maximus to his men.

Gladiator

'First we write with our head, then we write with our heart.'

Forrester to aspiring writer Jamal.

Finding Forrester (N.B. **not** a sequel to Finding Nemo and Dory)

'Mm! That is a tasty burger.'

Hitman Jules trying his victim's Wendy burger just before he shoots him.

Pulp Fiction

'Snakes, why did it have to be snakes?'

Indiana Jones on seeing what pesky critters he must overcome to find the Ark of the Covenant.

Raiders of the Lost Ark

There are loads of great lines in movies really. Dialogue is one of the things I love about these cinematic tales. Our older daughter Amy very recently quoted the one to me from *While You Were Sleeping*. The protagonist Lucy is commenting on a flashback about her childhood, and she throws in this line about how orange it all looks. She also says that when her father told her life doesn't turn out the way you expect, she didn't realise he was talking about *her life.*

The line from *Cinderella Man* is a great dad moment. It's the Great Depression and Jay is scared his parents will send him and the other children away for lack of food, so he has stolen some. His dad Jim tells him it's never right to steal, and then he promises Jay they will never, ever send him away. Beautiful. I have often referenced it when talking of God as a good and compassionate father, with his affirming and guiding love for us.

'Frankly my dear, I don't give a... BLEEP!'

This line is from *Gone with the Wind*, an epic I have to confess to not seeing. It's four hours long, isn't it? That aside, there is a story that goes with the line above. When the censors saw the scene where Rhett Butler says this line to Scarlett, they immediately yelled, 'Cut!' or something like that. They didn't like the ripe language when Rhett uses the word, '...damn.' The director George Cukor promised to drop the line. Then went ahead and left it in.

How times have changed. There are some scenes where I long for the actors to use the word 'damn' – rather than the 'a' 'b' 'c' 'd' 'f' or 's' words. (You can work them out if you need to, but I wouldn't bother.) Nowadays the f-word is called the f-bomb, but that's just to make it sound cooler, if you ask me. I'm sometimes asked about the language and other extreme elements in the films I watch. And frankly my dear, it's a problem. A lot of viewers don't even hear it, we're so used to it now. But I grew up in a house where swearing was not a good thing, and looking back, I'm glad. That said, when I was at school I swore like... well... a schoolboy. Though the words never felt comfortable in my mouth, a bit like trying to gargle with marbles I suppose.

As a writer I think it often weakens the dialogue. When you watch the old highly-rated classics there is little offensive language on offer. Oh, and I've recently noticed that Netflix have started warning of 'foul' language in some of their films rather than 'strong' language. Thumbs up to that. I hate the notion that swearing is considered strong when in reality it's weak most of the time. That said many of my favourite films contain plenty of swearing – *Goodfellas, Pulp Fiction, Withnail and I, The Departed, Love Actually* – to name just a few. But I would still rather they didn't. *Goodfellas* is based on Henry Hill's memoir and that book contains barely any bad language at all.

Paul, that great biblical writer, told his readers to think on things that are noble, true, pure, right, admirable and lovely. (Philippians 4 v 8) However, he did use the word for excrement when describing his past achievements. I'm with Paul, of course I am, but at the end of the day life is dark and difficult and littered with unnecessary things. Sometimes swearing in films illustrates this fact, sometimes I could do without it. It is comedies that I mostly take issue with, I find swearing unfunny in most of them. Ho hum. C'est la vie. And sadly it is *la vie*, so we each do our bit to steer a course through it.

Dick Clement and Ian La Frenais, the writers of the sitcom *Porridge*, invented their own words for comic effect – 'naff off' became the go-to expletive for prison inmates Fletch and Godber. I like that sort of creativity and have occasionally resorted to lines like – 'I don't give a flying fag end!' or 'What the frappuccino!?!' Years back a friend and I thought the word 'window' had a certain ring to it, as in 'You window!' You can put a bit of feeling into it. If you are writing comedy and can make people laugh about strange, bad language then perhaps you're making a point. Or something.

Awards Shmawards!

I can't help but get a little bit excited when the January to April awards season comes around. Though goodness knows why. These sharabangs are littered with disappointments and/or movies I've never heard of. From time to time I get lucky and a film I like takes home a trinket or two. My favourite season was 2017 – when I first started hearing about a little film called *La La Land*. There was a buzz around it as it had won every award it had been nominated for at the Golden Globes. It had an unusual title too and didn't sound like your average awards-worthy drama. The buzz went on growing over the following weeks as it continued winning, and of course the big prize is always the Oscar. Eventually the whole shebang climaxed with Bonnie and Clyde (a.k.a. Faye Dunaway and Warren Beatty) being given the wrong card and awarding *La La Land* the highly-prized best picture Oscar. Just as expected. That is until one of the producers, on a crowded, bustling stage, held up the right card and corrected the mistake so that *Moonlight* won.

There was another close call in 1985, the year that *Amadeus* won. Laurence Olivier was supposed to announce the nominees in alphabetical order but instead just read the first name on the list as the winner. Fortunately the actual winner, *Amadeus*, began with an A, so it topped the list of nominees and Sir Laurie had managed to call it correctly. Thank goodness it wasn't *Zootropolis*. Ironically, Olivier had been given a supreme introduction by Jack Lemmon, so much so that Olivier said he hoped he would be able to follow it by not letting the proceedings down too badly. He almost did!! You can hear a gasp as he starts to announce the winner rather than the nominees. *The Killing Fields* was also a runner that year and it's since become a favourite of mine. So I have to say, I'm disappointed with hindsight!

Disappointment is the one guaranteed thing about the Oscars. I've never quite recovered from *Forrest Gump* beating *Pulp Fiction*. And though *Schindler's List* won seven awards, including best picture and director for Spielberg, I'm still gutted that Liam Neeson, Ralph Fiennes and Embeth Davidtz were denied awards for their extraordinary performances. There *have* been moments of joy though. In spite of the fact that most critics think *Brokeback Mountain* should have won in 2004, I really like the winner *Crash*. I think the way it keeps wrongfooting the viewer is so clever. *Spotlight* too was a surprising win, but a great movie about fighting to bring light into darkness. *Chariots of Fire* deserves a mention, it won best picture (yay!), against all odds, but lost out in the best director category. This seems to happen with British directors. *Gladiator* won, but not the director Ridley Scott. *12 Years a Slave* won, but not the director Steve McQueen.

A long time ago in a year far, far away, I wrote the following, a piece about the way they always seemed to give the Oscar to the wrong actor for the wrong film. It's a bit of hokum really, but it was my way of expressing frustration a little...

And the Oscar Goes to...

At the American Academy Awards Ceremony this year they gave an Oscar to Kevin Spacey, who should have won one in 1998 for L.A. Confidential, the year they gave it instead to Jack Nicholson who should have won in 1992, the year they gave it instead to Gene Hackman who should have won in 1988, the year they gave it to Dustin Hoffman, who also won in 1979 the year they should have given it to Jack Lemon, who instead won in 1973 when Al Pacino should have won, who also should have won in 1990 the year they gave it to Jeremy Irons, who should have won in 1986, when they gave it to Michael Caine, who should really have won last year when they gave it to Roberto Benini who also beat Nick Nolte who should have won in 1991 the year they gave it to Anthony Hopkins who should have won in 1995 the year they gave it to Tom Hanks who certainly shouldn't have won again in 1996, the year they should have given it to John Travolta who's never won, just like Ralph Fiennes who should have won it in 1994 the year they gave it to Tommy Lee Jones who should have won it in 1991 the year they gave it to Jack Palance and the same year that Paul Newman should have won, instead they gave it to him in 1986 when William Hurt should have won, and they gave it to him in 1985 when Jon Voight should have won, and they gave it to him in 1978 when Robert De Niro should have won, but they honoured him in 1980 when Peter O'Toole should have won, but like Richard Burton, Tim Robbins, Tom Cruise, Liam Neeson, Alec Guinness, Albert Finney, Edward Norton, Ralph Fiennes, Jim Carrey, and a host of other talented actors - he's never won... unlike Woody Allen who's nominated every year in some category or other but always stays away, as did George C. Scott when he actually won in 1970 and Marlon Brando in 1972, who incidentally should have won in 1989 the year they gave it to Denzel Washington who should have won this year – but instead, they gave it to Kevin Spacey, who should have won in 1998 for L.A. Confidential...

As I say, a bit of hokum really. As is the whole awards season. At the end of the day, to misquote Julia Roberts in *Notting Hill*, 'It's all nonsense, nonsense it all is.' How can one person's performance in a screwball comedy be compared to another person's role in a harrowing drama? I think they should give at least twenty acting awards each year. Five for each category of male and female actors, leading and supporting. And that still wouldn't be enough. Roles and films often get overlooked simply because the makers don't have the funds to campaign and get noticed. I read recently that Harvey Weinstein managed to get *Shakespeare in Love* a best picture Oscar over *Saving Private Ryan* because he went round schmoosing the voters, whereas Mr Spielberg refused to do that. In the end Spielberg won best director for his war epic. Ultimately a film winning any award means it can then be forever known as 'the award-winning...' And maybe what it actually won for matters less over time. When we hear the phrase 'Oscar winning...' we may well think it won for best picture of the year.

Lately the viewing numbers are in decline, so there is some debate about the relevance of big awards ceremonies. Do we really need to see big stars pat each other on the back and hug their trophies? What matters more to us is seeing entertaining, thrilling and thoughtful films. That said, I did enjoy Brad Pitt's speech at the Screen

Actors Guild Awards when he won best supporting actor for *Once Upon a Time in Hollywood.* 'Each of us know pain and loneliness... we know moments of grace, we've had moments of wisdom... we've laughed at our ridiculousness and we know funny... and we bring all that to the screen.' It seems to me we bring all these things to our God too, articulated in lives offered as expressions of our faith and our worship as we bumble through each day, following Jesus.

And like the claim I mentioned earlier about some films being more 'important' than others, at the end of the day we can make up our own minds. We get to award our own Oscars. And perhaps we should be giving them to the folk we know who tirelessly help others. Who keep on encouraging us. Who stick by us whatever. Who don't get the limelight for all the great and wonderful things they do. I think that kind of award is what Jesus means when he talks about God knowing all we do, seeing the secret ways we reach out and help others. The small and great ways we make a difference. That's treasure in heaven. An Oscar in paradise.

Blue Like Jazz.

In recent years there has been a rise in faith-based films, in other words movies that communicate an explicitly Christian message. I have not seen many of these but you can find a list at www.sharefaith.com, or you can Google 'faith-based films.' (Other search engines are available.) You'll find titles like *Heaven is for Real, Miracles from Heaven, Faith Like Potatoes, Facing the Giants, God's Not Dead, Fireproof, Risen, The Shack* and *Little Boy*. These are big business in America now I believe, with so many churches having projectors and screens that these pictures don't need a cinema release in order to find a large audience. Some of them are made by Hollywood actors and filmmakers who cross back and forth between the two markets. I have seen *Miracles from Heaven* and also *The Shack* (based on the hugely popular novel). I found both of these extraordinarily moving. But my favourite is *Blue Like Jazz*.

Back in 2003 Don Miller wrote his book, *Blue Like Jazz*, it was subtitled *Non-religious thoughts on Christianity* and drew on his own story. A part of the book was about his time at Reed College, and in 2012 that part of the book became a film. The book has a humorous approach and this bleeds into the movie as well. Rather than it being a tale of plain sailing, it is about a young student trying to flee his faith. It's honest, shocking and funny, and has a wonderful closing scene. It manages to avoid platitudes and instead highlights the problems of life and faith. It plunges the faith into a world of questions, mistakes and popular culture.

It seems to me that anyone attempting a play, film, novel or short story about Christianity is doubly hampered. It's a challenge anyway to create a good, readable or watchable story about anything. But when talking, acting or writing about God and his presence in the world... well that's a bigger challenge again. Films and other art forms are not sermons. And what plays out with absolute authenticity in life can appear contrived and glib on a screen. CS Lewis's Narnia series is perfect because it's allegorical. It's not about God and Jesus and conversion and repentance and faith. It's about a family and a wardrobe and Turkish Delight and a witch in a castle and a powerful but wonderfully good lion. So it works perfectly as a great adventure and it's up to us to make the connections.

Conversion is one of the more difficult things to portray, and for my money the scene in Tom Hooper's *Les Misérables* is one of the best. Jean Valjean wrestles in song in the Bishop's chapel, effectively tussling with God's call on his life. He kneels in the semi-darkness, questioning who he is and what he's done. 'Is there another way to go?' he asks, tussling with his fear and his sin. And as he walks out into the graveyard, he flings the pieces of his parole document into the air, the music crescendos and the bells ring out. Valjean is ready to start his life again. The following story bears out this transformation. He has been offered forgiveness and grace, so reaches out in love and grace to those around him. So much so that his enemy Javert is overwhelmed, and unlike Jean Valjean, cannot bring himself to surrender to the grace of God.

The Sting.

We're big fans of the BBC series *Hustle* in our house. A series where a gang of con artists scam various unlikeable, well-dodgy rascals out of an awful lot of money. 'Never con an honest man,' is one of their sayings. The clever thing about this series is that we the viewers are often conned too. We are not given all the facts as we watch the story unfold, and often, just as we fear our heroes are going to be found out, or beaten up, or scammed themselves... bosh! We find there is more going on. I love that. I have always loved tales with a twist. I blame a short film called *An Occurrence at Owl Creek Bridge*, a story which ends in an unexpected way. We were shown this in an English class when I was about fourteen. I equally blame *Charade*, a fab 1960s film I saw around the same time, starring Cary Grant and Audrey Hepburn. A whodunnit by another name. Another twisty-turny, pull-the-rug kind of story.

But to return to *Hustle* for a moment. In one episode a member of the gang practically re-enacts one of Jesus's tales from Luke 16. Whilst recovering in hospital Albert gets bored, so he dons a white coat, pretends to be a hospital official and starts visiting other patients. He tells them he can handsomely reduce their fees if they pay him there and then in cash, which of course they do. Next thing you know Albert is sitting up in bed counting his spoils. Jesus tells a yarn about an employee who gets fired because of rumours of misconduct. (Only rumours though.) So the employee goes round to the company's customers reducing everyone's outstanding bills, and thus making friends with all those poor folk who owe his boss. It's a complex story, but the star of this show is really the money. The employee uses cash for good purposes, and everyone comes out looking good. The Boss appears generous, the employee brings good news, and those struggling with debt have less to pay. Money is used here to bless them all. Generosity saves the day. Use money in good ways, Jesus seems to be saying, don't let it misuse you.

But on to *The Sting*. Ah. Just brilliant. The unbelievably cool Redford and Newman scam their way through a meandering, feelgood, period yarn. I can't really tell you too much, better to watch it and get enthralled. *Hustle* has borrowed from it on several occasions. One thing we often miss in the gospels is that Jesus loved a twist in his tales. We may know his stories so well we fail to see how jaw-dropping they were. The Samaritans are now a really excellent organisation you can call when in a bad way. They are named after the parable of the Good Samaritan. But Jesus didn't give it that title. He didn't give it a title at all. He just started telling his story with a sting. I'm told that the plot construction was familiar. A priest, a Levite and a regular Joe. The priest was well within his rights not to help a bloodied and injured man, because he was washed and prepared for his temple duties and could not sully himself. The Levite was serving the priest and would have followed his lead. So it's down to the regular Joe.

Or rather a regular Israelite... BUT – WAIT! A regular Samaritan?? No! Really?? You're having a laugh! Aren't you? Two things. One – Samaritans were despicable low-life, and in those days it was quite acceptable to despise them. And two – the only Samaritan on that road would have been a soldier. And soldiers were unclean. (Notice that John the Baptist breaks all protocol by baptising soldiers in Luke 3.) So the hero here is doubly 'orrible. And yet... and yet... the Samaritan who stops to help stumps up good money, *and* risks his life to help this poor Jew. And risk his life he certainly did. If he took the man to a local inn there was every chance that a local posse would have gathered outside waiting to beat him up when he came out again. It's hard to come up with a contemporary equivalent because our cultural approach is different now. We might say a member of ISIS perhaps? Someone we fear and loathe. I did come across comments on a website which described a member of ISIS becoming a Christian. Some people applauded and were pleased, but there were others who refused to believe it.

'Blessed are the poor.' Another of Jesus's tale-twisty comments. Really? How? How does that work? Surely if you're rich you're blessed. God is clearly on your side giving you lots of stuff. Well... apparently not. When Jesus talks of a rich man blessed with abundant crops he then announces that man is a fool who deserves to die. Why? Because he's a waste of space. He won't share what he has. Just stores up his wealth. Later when Jesus is watching people putting their offerings into the temple treasury, he comments that a poor widow with barely two coins to rub together is blessed. Because her heart is in the right place. Her focus is clear.

Hitchcock and Humanity.

I have been a fan of Alfred Hitchcock's movies ever since I caught chickenpox back in 1987. Obviously he had nothing to do with me getting ill, I was working at Lee Abbey in Devon at the time and I think I caught it from a visiting guest. I went home to my parents for three weeks as I was feeling pretty rough, and whilst at home I found my dad had taped a collection of Mr H's classics on video. (Remember those VHS days?) So I worked my way through the collection – *Vertigo, Rear Window, Suspicion, Rope, The Trouble with Harry, Notorious, The Man Who Knew Too Much, Psycho.* I remember particularly liking *The Trouble with Harry*, a kooky comedy about a troublesome body being buried and dug up several times.

I have occasionally drawn on a scene from *Rear Window*, a voyeuristic thriller in which broken-legged cameraman James Stewart studies his neighbours through his long-range lens. One scene opens with the camera panning along the windows opposite his apartment on a hot day, and we see the neighbours all doing their thing. But then the camera continues panning and it comes round to James Stewart and we discover – horror of horrors – he is kissing Grace Kelly! The kissing is not so much the horror of it – it's the realisation that *we* are the voyeurs, not James. We thought he was scanning the neighbourhood, but it turns out he was otherwise engaged. It was us. We were spying on people.

At the start of the book of Amos the prophet tricks people with a not dissimilar manoeuvre.

He reels off a long list of Israel's enemies, detailing how they will get their comeuppance, and presumably his audience whoop and cheer with each pronouncement. But then, Amos suddenly switches and brings the camera onto them. Suddenly it's Israel and Judah who will get their comeuppance! Why? Because they've been busy leering at other nations and cheering their downfall instead of reaching out to them. They've been applauding instead of offering a hand of friendship. Judging rather than rescuing. They are caught out. Their misdemeanours are held up for them to see. So what will they do? Hear and respond? Stand there scratching their heads while their cheeks burn with embarrassment?

Perhaps there is a foreshadowing here of James's warning, early in his letter, that it's easy to look in the mirror then walk away and forget what you've seen, doing nothing about changing. Michael Jackson sang about a man in the mirror asking him to make a change. Not easy that. Whilst on a working trip to Kenya our group went on a safari. I spent the journey with my head out of the roof of the vehicle, partly to take in the view and partly because my confidence was at such a low ebb I couldn't face sitting in a confined space with relative strangers for an extended period. What I didn't realise was that my features were turning a darker shade of grit. When I looked in the mirror later I discovered my face was plastered with dust. Ouch! Did I feel a fool? Could Dumbo fly? Oh dear. I still wince at the thought now. I certainly made a change that day. But there are plenty of days when I look at myself but don't see myself. Too many preconceptions in the way.

Change is hard, to coin an understatement. Lasting change is anyway. Yet we are called into this life of slow transformation, even if the change is uphill, the road we are on is one that meanders towards something better. The irony is that we will always need Jesus, always have days, moments, weeks, hours, years of being that sheep wandering away. Just yesterday I saw a short film on social media of a sheep being hauled out of a narrow ditch by its back legs. The thing then immediately went skipping off only to fall straight back into the ditch further down the road! That's us. Me anyway.

Hitchcock, who was known as the master of suspense, was once asked if he was actually afraid of anything himself. He replied that he was afraid of plenty of things, which was why he could make such terrifying films. He knew what fear was. He had experienced terror and so could recreate that for others. Who'd have guessed? It's easy to look at others and think they are infallible experts. Superhuman perhaps, above normal experience. But we are all human. Various artists and actors have said in interviews that they fear being 'found out', being unmasked, perhaps, as frauds – not great artists or actors after all. We do well to avoid putting people on pedestals. Hitch was as easy to scare as the rest of us. In fact his knowledge and experience of fear was what made him a great filmmaker. Weakness is a shared language, isn't it? And a powerful one too. It taps into the very heart of what it is to be human, though it's a costly language to use. It leaves us vulnerable and open to criticism. Which is why artists often express their troubles and weaknesses through their art. It's why Jesus used stories to unlock the people he met. He knew that those with open ears, eyes and hearts would find themselves in his profound tales and make a response. On one occasion a bunch of uppity religious folks got all upset by one of his stories. Not because he had accused them of anything, but they saw themselves in the tale and were challenged. (Have a look at Mark chapter 12 verse 12.)

I wonder when a story last affected you in some way? I watched an episode of *Downton Abbey* a while back, one in which a character grew ill and died. Watching the reaction of the family and servants was powerful. The story has stayed with me. We live in a frightening and difficult world. You don't need me to tell you that. One of the great things about prayer is that we can express our fears and anxieties. Prayer is not about having great faith and answers. It's about a growing relationship. An honest struggle, a wrestling match with life, the world, ourselves and God. As Jacob found at the river Jabbok in Genesis chapter 32 verses 22-31. We can bring our hopes, longings, questions, anger, frustrations, courage, doubts and terrors. We can lay it all out. Knock, knock, knocking on heaven's door. Using whatever words or silence or songs help us. And to quote a famous, deeply honest prayer from someone who came to Jesus when life was hard and fearful. 'I believe, but I also doubt, help me in my unbelief.' (Mark chapter 9 verse 24.)

Woofers and Tweeters?

I don't only refer to films in my talks and presentations about the Bible, I also draw on news stories, comedy sketches and TV programmes. So here's an unexpected way to draw near the end of this part of the book. Not a reflection on a movie, but a comedy moment. I came across this classic *Hi Fi Shop* sketch recently when watching a documentary about the *Not the Nine O'clock News* team. Known as the *Woofers and tweeters sketch* (you'll see why) a guy walks into a shop looking to buy the latest music machine (this was back in the 1980s) and the two hip young dudes behind the counter use their technical know-how to make him feel like an idiot. 'D'you want a Dolby with it? D'you want rumble filters? D'you want woofers and tweeters? D'you want a bag on your head?' As the man flounders at each question, the youngsters fall about laughing from their place of coolness and power. It's a smart and funny piece and the odd thing is, the customer might appear to lack knowledge, but it's the two behind the counter who look really ignorant.

When chatting with my wife Lynn about it we started to talk about those times when you feel out of your depth. This poor guy walks into a Hi Fi shop wanting to buy a 'gramophone' only to find himself torn to shreds by the hip dudes behind the counter. I have sometimes felt a little like this when wandering into unknown situations. I know nothing about DIY or cars and so sometimes feel out of my depth when needing to get one fixed. Not that I've ever been treated like the poor guy in the sketch, I must add. I've always found those in the know to be helpful, kind and understanding. But knowledge is power, isn't it? And we can either wield it like an offensive weapon or use it to help each other. 'Truth is like a blanket that always leaves your feet cold.' I mentioned this line earlier, Ethan Hawke says it in *Dead Poets Society*. Truth without kindness can be cruel. We can use it to assert ourselves, to make ourselves strong while weakening others.

The extraordinary thing about Jesus is he had all the knowledge in the universe and yet never used it as a weapon. He preferred grace and generosity. He welcomed the nervous and hesitant and drew them into his new kingdom with entertaining stories and random acts of compassion. He never bludgeoned or pressurised anyone. 'Come to me and it will be like finding a place to rest and recuperate,' he said. Like a refreshing drink on a baking hot day. (Have a look at Matthew 11 v 28 and John 7 v 37-38.) He wasn't offering regulations and religion. A stifling experience which made you feel like an idiot if you got it wrong. He'd come to help those who felt weak or foolish. He was wooing us towards a life that would build us up, not tear us down. The weary and the lost and the wayward and the incompetent found a home with him. We still do.

Chariots of Fire.

I was only 18 when I first saw *Chariots of Fire* and wasn't immediately blown away by it. These days it is a film I love and will watch again and again and again. It's not easy to portray good people on screen, that's why so many villains win Oscars. Hannibal the Cannibal, Gordon Gecko, Nurse Ratched, The Joker (twice). You can really get your teeth into a baddie. Goodness is more of a challenge. Ian Charleson managed to capture the essence of Scottish athlete Eric Liddell without making him appear overly pious, though the story was tweaked to add some extra drama. (Liddell was so clear-sighted and focussed about his life and faith that he didn't need to wrestle with running on a Sunday.)

There is a great moment when Liddell is about to run the 400m final. As they line up for the race, one of the American runners hands him a piece of paper. Liddell unfolds it and reads the following.

'It says in the old book, "He that honours me I will honour." Good luck, Jackson Scholz.' It's a perfect reminder of something Liddell had said earlier to his sister.

'When I run I feel God's pleasure.'

Liddell honoured God with his gift, and God honoured him. There is an old saying, attributed to a guy called Irenaeus, 'The glory of God is a human being fully alive.' When Eric ran he was showing something of God's glory, doing what he loved and what he was designed to do.

My wife and older daughter love watching *The Great Pottery Throwdown*, where contestants work with clay each week. One of the judges, Keith, loves what the contestants make, so much so that from time to time he cries, he is so moved by their work. Recently I was watching a film on YouTube about the making of Ian Dury's song *Hit Me With Your Rhythm Stick*. The presenter Warren, breaks down classic songs and talks about how they were made and how they have influenced other musicians. Towards the end of this short film he began to say how much he loved this song... and he started to well up and had to stop for a moment. He was clearly very moved.

John Mark Comer, in his book *Garden City*, describes the feeling he got when seeing a sunset, and sensing God's glory. But then he got the same feeling when he looked at a beautifully made cabinet. It was if this piece of furniture had been made so well, that it spoke of God's glory. I think that is why Keith and Warren are moved by pottery and songs. It may sound strange, but even if we cannot put it into words, the glory of God can still speak through someone doing something they love. Doing it with all their heart.

Early in *Chariots* Eric's father tells him that, '...you can praise the Lord by peeling a spud, if you peel it to perfection!' I'm not sure you have to peel it to perfection, just as well as you can. Everything can give God glory. We can honour him in the washing up and cleaning of loos. In the ordinary and extraordinary. He's a 24/7 God.

There's another line which comes to mind.

'Life slips by, Abrahams, life slips by.'

So says the Master of Trinity college to Harold Abrahams, as they discuss studying, honour and running.

Time moves relentlessly forward and there is no great stick we can jam in the spokes to stop the movement of it. I saw a sign in a window a while back that said, *Try not to take life too seriously, no one gets out alive.* However, the great Christian hope is that this life is not the be-all-and-end-all. There is more. This is no vague hope, but one clearly defined, crafted and offered by the man from Nazareth. In his life, actions, death and resurrection, Jesus has opened a new way for us. He encouraged his friends by promising that his living, dying and rising were like the actions of a dedicated bridegroom, building brand new rooms on his father's ever-expanding house, an endless number where new and eternal life could take place. What we might call *Life in Technicolour,* to quote the title of a song by the band Coldplay. And this is not a fingers-crossed kind of hope, but a hope born out of trusting in this man who spent his long and busy days offering his life for others.

I am often not full of faith, I can worry and doubt for England. But my heart is warmed as I listen to the words of Jesus, as I think on the smile of that man, the hands extended to the lost and worried. 'I have come to bring you life,' he said, 'life in all its fullness.' I don't know what that will look like, but I hang on to that great hope, often described as a 'sure hope'. The hope of Jesus.

And so to finish, a short reading:

The Hills We Must Climb

He is with us on the hills we climb,

(Often feeling like mountains to us)

Hills we cannot avoid,

Hills of our own making,

The hills thrust upon us.

The demands and pressures we face,

Those things we must do,

The struggles in our mind,

Never-ending repeated tasks of the day,

He is with us on the hills we must climb.

In the valleys that appear

To have no end anytime soon,

The tunnels where the light

Seems very distant indeed,

The days that feel so full of travelling

With no arrival in sight.

Our Desert Son is used to these hills,

The potholed lanes and winding paths,

The transfiguring climbs and

The calvary roads, these ways of life.

He knows the hills we must climb,

And never leaves us to travel alone.

Movies You Love or Find Inspiring.

Feel free to make your own list and notes here.

Some Short Movie Reflections Which May Be Useful

To find out more about each film it's probably best to look them up on the IMDB website (The Internet Movie Data Base) – IMDB.com.

Red Joan

When Joan Stanley gets a knock at the door one day she opens it to find a huddle of cops on the doorstep. She is under arrest. For spying. Surely not. Not this quiet unassuming lady in this quiet unassuming house. And so we follow her back in time to Cambridge, and her days as a brilliant student, befriended by the mysterious and impassioned Sonya and Leo. As times go by she becomes a Government civil servant, and part of the team developing the science for the atomic bomb. But Sonya and Leo keep reappearing in her life, bringing pressure to bear on her about 'sharing information'. Joan gets increasingly caught up in events beyond her control.

Do spies ever see themselves as spies? Obviously James Bond does, because in his world spies are suave and sophisticated. In real life, one would imagine, the more ordinary they look the better. They need to blend in, go unnoticed. The Bible features a couple of spies in the book of Joshua (chapter 2), they sneak over the wall into the Promised Land to check things out. But trouble comes their way, there is a mole who rats on them (to mix my furry creature metaphors for a moment), soon they are in grave danger, and it takes an unexpected hero to rescue them. Rahab hides the spies and provides a cover story for them in return for the promise of safety for her family in the coming days. She doesn't realise it but her brief moment in the spotlight is going down in history. In two ways. Rahab is listed in Hebrews chapter 11 verse 31 as being a woman of faith because of her courage and trust here. But also, her son Boaz grows up to marry another hero – Ruth. And as such Rahab will be the great, great, great, great, great, great etc... grandmother of Jesus himself. How about that? The woman who brought rescue to two spies, became part of the family of the son who would rescue the world. We never know how our actions, how our kindness, encouragement and courage, might help others.

Made in Italy

There is a saying – wherever you go, there you are. You cannot escape yourself. And it is certainly true of father and son Robert and Jack, when they head off to Italy to sell the villa that belonged to Robert's wife. Their relationship is not in the best of health, plus son Jack needs to sell this house because his marriage is crumbling and he is desperate to buy the art gallery where he works in London. So the two guys pitch up at the most dust-ridden and cobwebbed villa you can imagine, in the most glorious setting you can imagine. (It made me wonder whether it's just us Brits who have a fascination with stories about nipping off to warmer climes to do things up.) And so, as they do battle with this behemoth of a property (complete with a massive angst-ridden red mural which Robert painted after he lost his wife) so they do battle with each other. There is much that has not been said over the years, and perhaps, as they splash paint about and extricate a hissing weasel which has taken up residence in the waterless bathroom, this will be the chance they need to truly talk.

Sometimes having something else to focus on can be the release mechanism for a little more honesty. I recall attending a writing workshop a few years back and hearing this enlightening piece of wisdom re constructing dialogue – people never really say what they mean. Later I came across another thought on writing, behind every sentence written (or spoken too, I guess) there are five more lines unsaid. So much goes on beneath the surface of our regular living. We do our best to appear in control, though we may well be floundering beneath the surface. This is where Jesus seems to excel with people. Reading between the lines. He could hear what was really being said in the banter and the small talk and the arguments. He understood the longings and fears tucked between the cliches and weather-talk. And still does. We can pray anything, no need to dress up our presentation or find the right words. Just talk.

Le Mans 66

When the brilliant Ken Miles is asked to slow down in the 24 hour Le Mans race so that his teammates can catch up with him and they can all cross the line together, he has a problem. He's not a team player anyway, and he is here to prove that he is the best. So he intends to ignore the request. But as he nears the finishing line, he has second thoughts, and amazes everyone by hitting the brake pedal. However, his wife Mollie, watching on their TV at home, nods to herself and whispers, 'Well done Ken.' She knows him, knows he's the best. Humility is a hard quality to quantify. Some fear that it turns us into a doormat. It's certainly not popular in the age we live in. Pride is what matters. Asserting yourself. Stating your case. And often forcing others aside to prove the point. When Jesus said, 'Blessed are the humble,' the word he used here summons up the image of a powerful horse under control. Another definition describes humility as knowing our place in the world, and being secure in that. In the letter to a bunch called the Philippians, Jesus is described as humble, giving up everything he had for us. And when he knelt to wash his friends' feet we are told that he wasn't trying to prove anything. He knew where he had come from, where he was going, and the immense power that God had given him. Being secure in this enabled him to kneel and wash feet. (You can read this in John chapter 13 verses 3-4.) This was humility for him. Knowing he was accepted, and valued, and cared for by God. I see something about humility in this moment from Le Mans. Mollie and Ken are at ease with each other, and with their world. When Ken was denied the chance to enter the race on another year, she brought him a beer, tuned the radio to some music and quietly danced with him. We need help to be humble, it's not always cultural, but it does make the world a better place.

A.I. Artificial Intelligence

When Monica and Henry 'adopt' the human robot David, they are given the option to programme, or imprint, him to love them. After a while Monica does just that, and from then on David is set on homing in on her and receiving her love. You get a sense of insecurity as he longs to be sure that she loves him as he loves her. One of the great themes of the Bible is that we have a creator, we are no accident, we are made in his image, with the capacity to begin to know our Maker and start to love him. However, unlike this story, we have freewill. It's one of the great gifts of life. We can choose how we live. We are not imprinted or programmed to love God, instead we have the choice to do this. Add into that the nature of the world we live in, broken, stressed and full of distractions... and life gets complex. For those who want to love God it's not easy. We love other things and let them dominate our thinking. We frequently forget the one who can help us in this fractured world. Like Monica with David, we are talking about a relationship, and one in which we feel frequently insecure. God will not always do what we want, and at times life feels like wading through wet cement.

The Bible is full of folk like us. And they do not hide their troubles and inadequacies. The book of Psalms is full of writing often referred to as songs of praise, but many of them are songs of lament, and cries for a better way of life. The writers pour out their longings and inadequacies. In Psalm 69 the writer tells us he is exhausted, worn out. He feels as if he is drowning, and he is worried that his foolish ways will cause others to come a cropper. This is honest stuff. Real faith, real life. We are not robots, we don't have it all worked out, and the great thing is that we can be honest with God about it.

Escape from Pretoria

This remarkable true story is all about keys. And the way political prisoner Tim Jenkin secretly fashioned a whole set in his cell. He and his friend were incarcerated in a South African high security prison for distributing anti-apartheid leaflets. For speaking up for truth and justice. But the resourceful pair refused to stay locked in, and hatched a plan so startling you'd think it ridiculous if it weren't true. Freedom is an elusive concept, even for those of us not held behind bars. It's hard to appreciate the freedom we have and things like money, lack of opportunity, broken dreams and other people can all seriously hem us in. It's worth remembering those who have lost their freedom because of their faith in Jesus. 260 million Christians live in countries where there can be circumstances of great threat and pressure. May we find moments today to appreciate the good things we have, and to pray for those who are struggling. Life is never perfect, we all know this, we live in a fractured world, and for some it is very difficult indeed. As we draw near Easter we remember that Jesus gave everything to bring freedom, and to inspire and empower us to live with the same desire and hunger for truth and justice that he had. Lord, help us appreciate life when it is hard to do so, and help us remember those for whom getting through each day is a challenge. Thank you, Amen.

The Highwaymen

There is a strange and unexpected moment in this movie about two Texas Rangers on the trail of Bonnie and Clyde. One of the rangers, Maney Gault, is hanging around in a side alley when he spots the outlaws' car turning off the high street and pulling up near him. A prime opportunity to finally nail the brutal couple. However, as he pulls his gun from its holster he hears the sound of screams and running feet and watches in disbelief as the car is surrounded by adoring fans. Bonnie had become so revered that women were dressing like her. And 20,000 people attended her funeral. The world seemed to have gone mad. What on earth were people thinking? And yet, in many ways we still do it. For example... we know more than ever how much the celebrity life can ruin people, and yet still want to be famous. We still idolise that which is destructive. Romanticising about lives other than our own. We have been constantly speaking of the new normal these past twelve months, well, maybe ordinary can be the new normal. Maybe regular is enough. 'Wherever you go, there you are.' We always take ourselves, and our quirks and fears and weaknesses, with us. Whether we are famous or not. When God entered this world he didn't come as a power-player, or a gangster, or a celebrity. He came as a nobody. A regular kid playing in the street. A strapped-for-cash carpenter labouring under high taxation. Perhaps he did that because he knew that this is the reality for most of us. Ordinariness. And reality was what was most important to him. Not some glamorous, fabricated existence. But life as it is, gritty, troublesome and a bit of a mishmash.

'God became a human being and moved into the neighbourhood. Full of love and faithfulness.' John 1 v 14

The Last Temptation

I'll be the first to admit that this film is strange in places, an unusual retelling of the life of Jesus. However, it also has some fantastic moments. Like the time Jesus spits into his hands so he can heal a man who can't see. You can find the account in John 9 v 6-7. It's the kind of scene that might make you want to go, 'Ugh!' Not a reaction you often get when the account is read in church. But the spit in this movie is real, gloopy, sticky stuff. Not some otherworldly, sparkly, shiny spit, with a bit of fairy dust sprinkled on top. This is the real deal. Because Jesus was fully human and fully alive. With real saliva in his mouth. I sometimes wonder whether I can be over-reverential in my faith, keeping God at a polite distance. And the thing is, God refused to keep his distance. He burst into the neighbourhood, into this world of sweat, stress, strain and spit. Looking all too genuinely earthy and earthly. Malcolm Muggeridge once said something like – religion can be our way of keeping God at bay. Well, he wouldn't be kept at bay. We were too important to him. You were too important to him. He wasn't afraid of our darkness or despair or duplicity, or demanding ways. This was God in jeans and a hoodie. Not looking like God at all. Instead spending his time laughing, crying, listening, transforming the lives of the lost and the ordinary and the loveless. Entrusting himself to us, and to every inch of our brilliant, grumpy, glorious, shambling, critical, cynical, money-haunted, sewer-strewn, hungry world. Oh yes.

Jojo Rabbit

At one point in this satirical tale set in war-torn Germany, Jojo's mother embarrasses him by jumping on a wall and dancing. She has of course no right to do this, partly because she is with her son who would rather she just behave properly in public, and mostly because they are losing the war and life is very precarious indeed. But she tells Jojo that people dance because they are free. Her dancing expresses her view on life. Even in dire circumstances she has hope. Later Jojo will be found dancing too. It seems that for his mother freedom is not so much about the tyranny of the situation she finds herself in, but her approach to life. Her worldview. And she is concerned to pass that on, not only to Jojo but to others too. At risk to her own safety and wellbeing. Jesus spoke of the truth that can set us free, and he was living in a time of oppression too. His friends were desperate to rid themselves of the chokehold the Romans had over them, but for Jesus freedom was about something else. Having spoken of the freedom truth could bring he then described himself as being the truth. He was hoping his friends would join the dots and make the connection. Jesus lived free, able to respond to situations and people with open hands. And like Jojo's mum, he was willing to risk everything to bring this freedom to others.

News of the World

Captain Kidd is an unusual news journalist. An ex-soldier he now travels the far flung towns and communities of post-civil war America telling recent news stories to those who have not yet heard them. He is a great storyteller and people give well to hear his reports of the serious and the strange and the unexpected. He holds his audience in the palm of his hand as he draws them in to hear what is going on beyond the borders of their own small worlds. I wonder whether storytelling of this sort is a bit of a lost art, in an age when CGI and TV on-demand can provide us with anything, we may have forgotten how powerful it can be when one person holds a live audience captive as they tell their gripping yarns. Jesus came from a culture of this kind of 'journalism'. He was a herald for the kingdom of

God, a kingdom which many had been misled about. He had come to open their eyes to the reality of this other dimension, which was accessible to all and closer than breathing. And so he told his thrilling tales of gangs abducting messengers, employees playing fast and loose with the boss's money, and sons running away to live the high life. These were no dull sermons, not at all, these were tales of the unexpected, twisting and turning before the wide-eyes of each expectant crowd. You didn't need wi-fi or a satellite dish or a widescreen telly. You just had to pause, lean in a little and let the stories grip your imagination. And unlike our fast-flowing torrent of modern entertainment, these tales stayed with you, you could retell them to others, and their impact might well be so huge you would never be the same again. This really was news of the world and I guess news for the world too. If you've not discovered them you could do worse than take a few moments to jump into the fast-paced Mark's gospel (or blog) in the world's number one bestseller, The Bible.

Greenland

In the new disaster movie *Greenland* a comet heads for the earth, and John Garrity receives a text telling him to take his family to an airbase in order to be flown to safety. Bits of the deadly missile are about to destroy entire cities. Massive traffic jams, looters and dodgy phone signals all conspire against their escape, and it's not long before the family are separated. As in so many films about catastrophe, lots of folk turn against one another in their bid to survive. But there is a lovely moment when John's son Nathan urgently needs supplies for his medical condition. Being unwell Nathan and his mother Allison are rejected from the flight to safety, as numbers are limited, but as they seek refuge in a makeshift shelter a nurse comes to their aid. She checks Nathan's condition and prepares the medical aid they need. She offers welcome help in a time when other doors are shutting all around them. I'm so grateful for those who have, to paraphrase Jesus, 'gone the extra mile' when I have needed it. Those who look for a way to bring a better moment, a better day for another. We have, I'm sure, all been inspired by those who have set their own agendas aside, and continue to do so, in this extreme and difficult time.

The Matrix

At one point in this mind-bending, reality questioning movie the hero Neo goes to visit the all-knowing Oracle, to see if he may be the one to free the earth from the grip of The Matrix. In the waiting room there he meets others who have been brought along to see if they are the appointed rescuer. It seems in movieland that people are often looking for a saviour. It happens in Harry Potter, Lord of the Rings, Narnia. As well as the Marvel, DC and Star Wars Universes. Harry's the one, no Frodo's the one, no Neo's the one. We're hardwired to want tales of a powerful saviour. Someone who can right the wrongs and set the world back on course. The unexpected thing about the Christian worldview is that there is a saviour, but he doesn't turn up with superpowers, able to dodge speeding bullets or perform gravity-defying kung fu. The Bible describes the weakness of God, assuring us that it is stronger than any earthly force. The weakness of God expressed in a hero who gives his life in the most cruel, embarrassing, unexpected of ways. Pinned up and looking like a failure. There were many looking for a rescuer in Jesus's day, apparently many boys were called Joshua in the hope that they might grow up to emulate the Old Testament hero and bring the people into a new kind of freedom. But they would never have imagined it to be a simple, highly compassionate carpenter from small town Nazareth. Never have foreseen that the way to bring new life was through the door of sacrifice and execution. Yet on a quiet Sunday morning the revolution they longed for began.

The Dig

Ralph Fiennes perfectly embodies the deferential, self-taught excavator Basil Brown, in this true story of the sensational archaeological dig at Sutton Hoo in the late 1930s. As war looms, he sets about unearthing what is beneath the burial mounds on Edith Pretty's land. She has wanted to know for a long time what might be found there. It's a tale shot through with the questions of life and death. Early on Edith tells Basil about the ancient finger marks found when the explorers first opened Tutankhamen's tomb, and she describes Brown's mission as 'digging down to meet the dead'. Later, Brown talks about the handprints we each leave behind in this life. Which is surely true. Fingerprint legacies. But is that the only way we live on? It seems to me that the great Christian hope is twofold... the presence of Jesus in our lives now to give us hope and help and purpose as we muddle through our days. And the enlarging of our worldview to encompass a whole other dimension and time frame beyond that which we can see or touch. We don't just live on through the footprints we leave in this world, but through Jesus we have the promise of a whole other life, not merely pie in the sky, but the ever-present dimension of the kingdom of God, a much larger world, full of peace and compassion, transformation and respect. An eternal life which will one day break fully into this transient life, and one which will never end.

Run Fatboy Run

In *Run Fatboy Run*, as Dennis attempts to run a marathon he has not really trained for, he hits a wall. And he can't break through it. So he is tempted to give up on the race. It would be easier to just walk away and give up trying. But as he looks at the wall he sees a vision of himself calling him on, telling him not to give up. So he starts again. Keeps going, albeit in a hobbling kind of way. We may frequently feel like throwing in the towel, we may feel out of shape for the challenges of this race of life. Unfair walls spring up to block our path, and we wonder how we'll keep going. We haven't trained for the challenges that we find ourselves facing. The writers of the

Bible describe life as a race, and they are well aware that we may often hit walls, or fall off the track. Which is why they remind us that those who have gone before, running this very race, are urging us on, saying, 'Don't give up! We made it and so can you.' Their voices may be heard through the messages from others. Emails, social media posts, phone calls, a smile or kind word from a passing friend or stranger. Which is why it's good to be kind. Be kind, be kind, be kind as Mr Rogers once said. Because we never know how our kindness might encourage someone who has hit a wall today. Someone who needs a kind nudge, a lift, to help them keep going.

'Let's keep running this chaotic race, urged on by the huge crowd of witnesses who have been this way before us... fixing our eyes on the One who has run before us and can help us with the troubles, burdens and distractions that weigh us down.' Hebrews 12 v 1-2

Rogue Warriors

Not a film this time, but a three-part series (shown on BBC iPlayer) about the remarkable story of the founding of the SAS in North Africa, in 1941. This documentary tells the unlikely tale of what happened when maverick David Stirling had the vision of a different kind of unit, one that would fight behind the enemy lines. He gathered together a bunch of incredibly courageous misfits and rebels, who were willing to live and do battle in the harshest conditions. In this very particular kind of role these men gave everything, and so the SAS was born.

It seems to me that the Old Testament is full of mavericks and misfits and rebels. People who have gone down in history for their faith and courage and determination in the most difficult of circumstances. Folks like Ruth, Daniel, Ezekiel, Esther, Rahab, David, Rizpah and Moses took incredible risks, laying everything on the line at times. Inspired and strengthened by their love for God and their devotion to others. That great saintly scribbler Paul wrote about the way God chooses the foolish folk to disrupt the wise. Inviting misfits and strugglers to follow him and be part of the work of love on this earth. Choosing the little people, to do small, remarkable things.

The Book of Eli

There is a moment towards the end of *The Book of Eli* when Eli is asked about the nature of the Bible he is carrying. He says this, 'It's beat up, but it will do the job.' He is actually not only referring to the Bible, but to himself. He is carrying the book in his memory, in his being, and he begins to recite it so it can be written down. This book is in essence alive, coursing through his veins, embedded in his DNA. Not because he's a saint or anything like that, but because he wants to carry it like this. And it's the case that he is beaten up, has been through many toils, snares and dangers. The Bible itself full of troubled people who have seen their fair share of difficulties. And they have drawn strength, hope and purpose from this Living Word. This Good Book provides many camera angles on life with God, and most of them are presented by folks who are struggling, oppressed and full of questions. Many of us are like Eli, we feel a bit bashed about, yet we can carry within us this living word, not because we are saints, but because we need it. The writer of Psalm 119 assures us that, 'Your word is a lamp to my feet and a light to my path' (verse 105). Or, as The Message version tells us – 'By your words I can see where I'm going; they throw a beam of light on my dark path.'

Three Billboards Outside Ebbing, Missouri

There are a few surprising happenings in this bitter, brutal film about a mother crying out for justice. Not least when the local advertising guy, Red Welby, finds himself in the next hospital bed to the wayward cop who beat him up. Part way through their conversation Red offers the badly injured cop a drink, and fetches him an orange juice with a straw turned towards him to make the drinking a little easier. A small yet tender offering in this dark tale. I'm reminded of the saying about the light shining brightly in the darkness, the acts of tenderness and compassion are unexpected here and stand out all the more against the stark backdrop of trouble and anger. We have recently celebrated Christmas, in a season of short days and long dark nights. And though the baubles and glitter are most prominent, it is of course a celebration of light breaking into the darkness. Not with Marvel superpowers, but in a profoundly small, tender and vulnerable way. The tiny light of God, needing feeding, clothing washing and loving. An inextinguishable candle. The kind of light that knows struggles and troubles. Plunged into our difficult world.

Dear Lord, you know better than us how dark the world can seem at times like this. Please help us to be a part of shining your light to help others, in Jesus's name, amen.

The Family Man

In the festive fave *It's a Wonderful Life* George wishes he'd never been born, and when an angel grants him that wish, he discovers how precious life is and what a positive difference he has made to others over the years. In the film *The Family Man*, self-satisfied high-flyer Jack meets an angel who gives him another kind of glimpse, he shows him what life would have been like if he'd loved people rather than wealth and power. Jack finds himself impoverished materially, but enriched like crazy in other more chaotic, more important ways. When the glimpse is over, like Scrooge, Jack is a changed man. Angels can appear in all kinds of guises to show us what matters in life. Sometimes in the words and actions of friends and strangers. I'll never forget the unexpected smile from a passing stranger which lifted my spirits no end, one weary day in London. Which of course does mean we may be an 'angel' for someone today, bring a smile, or a kind word or act to another. We never know what folks are living with or going through, and how much we have the power in our hands to make life a little better for them.

Lord, please help us to bring your kindness to others today, even if we are not aware of it, Amen.

Little Women

Not exactly a Christmas film, but one that features two Christmases in it! I love the 1995 version of this tale, and find it deeply moving. Not least the scene where Beth, in her final moments, assures her sister Jo that she is not afraid. Her three sisters have great ambition and have been off on their various adventures, but for the first time Beth is going ahead of them. To a new place. And she is not frightened. She has a gentle assurance about the next life. One of the great promises of Jesus is that his death and resurrection pave the way for a new life after this one. The assurance that there is more to come. He has gone ahead of us. There is a saying that this life is not a rehearsal and in many ways it is true. But this life is also only the first act in an endless, timeless epic. 'I'm going away to prepare a place for you,' Jesus assured his friends in John chapter 14. In this life we live with trouble and great loss. And Jesus lived with that himself. But in him we can take hope, and cling on to the promise of a full life to come.

Lord, please help us when we need assurance, thank you for all you have prepared for us. Amen.

Home Alone

When a couple of pesky burglars do their utmost to break into young Kevin's house, our optimistic hero has to do battle with them, using any means at his disposal, along with all the ideas and courage he can muster. It's another David and Goliath tale, Kevin really shouldn't triumph in this one-sided contest. And though both stories involve startling violence, ultimately Kevin's yarn and David's adventure are both tales of an underdog winning out with creativity, guts and clear thinking. Teenager David refuses the standard fighting gear and posture, and instead relies upon a/ keeping his distance, b/ the catapult that fits his style perfectly, and c/ his faith in a God bigger than any sneering brute leering across any valley. We face many giants, in many forms, and they can be intimidating and belittling. Let's face it, life is fraught with challenges. Not least at the moment. May we find what we need in the words David utters as he squares up to the giant in his life – 'I'm here in the name of the Lord God.'

Lord, please give us the courage, the stamina, the hope and the vision we need for this day. Not because our faith is great, but because You are. Amen.

Bridge of Spies

There is a telling moment towards the end of Spielberg's espionage thriller, *Bridge of Spies*, a moment I missed on first viewing. Lawyer James Donovan has just returned from a trip to East

Germany, where he has witnessed the building of the Berlin wall, and he is now travelling back through free America on a train. Looking out at life he sees a group of youngsters hurl themselves at a fence and clamber happily over it. The last time he saw a group of people do that they were attempting to get over the Berlin wall and were gunned down in the process. It's a brief moment but the contrast is stark and it reminds me of a couple of things.

Freedom is precious, and I so easily take it for granted. Reminders like this can be important and helpful, we all struggle with life not being as we would like it, but there are many who live under strict regimes.

Secondly, it's hard to appreciate the good things we have, I find reminders like this come and go too quickly. For a moment I'm grateful, but then my thoughts move on. And sometimes when we hear of others' difficulties we know we should be thankful, but still find it hard to do that. I want to be grateful, I want to remember the good things, but the bad things crowd them out. That prolific letter writer Paul, wrote in his letter to the Philippians that he had learnt to be happy with what he had, a lot or a little. It's a useful nudge. Contentment can seem like a bar of soap. Grasp it for a moment then – whoops – it's gone.

Military Wives

As a group of wives and their families await the return of their loved ones from the fighting in

Afghanistan, they find various ways of counting the days. Homemade calendars, tick boxes, jars of depleting sweets... and they keep busy too. Though they are a disparate bunch, reluctant and cautious at first, they form a ragtag choir, and at times they surprise themselves with what is possible. However, this is not so much about aspiring to great musical things, but sharing support and friendship as they wait. That's what is really important here. Because the waiting is hard, any phone call or text message could bring bad news. But they hold on, and they help each other to hold on.

Believe it or not the Bible is full of people waiting. Posh-coated Joseph spending years in prison. Jacob working for a decade or more for his beloved Rachel. Moses chasing sheep around the desert for 21,024,000 minutes wondering where things went wrong. Anna waiting a lifetime to hold the baby from Bethlehem and see hope in his tiny glistening eyes. And then there are those blank pages. The 400 years between the Old and New Testaments. We read of Malachi's promise of a new dawn, bringing light and healing; justice, laughter and joy (Malachi chapter 4). And then... a gap. (Though of course some Bibles include the Apocrypha here.) It's easy to flick over these two blank pages in our Bibles, they are very thin after all, but they represent centuries of hoping. Till eventually... one day an angel appears to an aging priest called Zechariah, in Matthew chapter 1, promising the impossible.

Life contains a lot of waiting when it boils down to it. And the sometimes-overlooked season of Advent is probably a lot more relevant than we realise. We want something better, something safer, some improvements. Something more. Please! We are not alone of course, for 2000 years Christians have been waiting for a new world, and it's been a busy waiting! I guess we're not supposed to hang around with our hands in our pockets looking up at the sky. That's why Luke wrote the book of Acts. Like the military wives we have things we can do. An active kind of waiting.

It has been said that God is in the waiting. God is in the trudgery. Which does not make it any easier, any rosier, any cooler. But he is here. And he understands. He waits too, for so many things. For a world to lift its head and look to him. For a day when the time is right for him to return and set things right. We wait. He waits. With us. Please help us Lord. With our emptiness and disappointments, and all that is unknown to us. And help us to help each other, though we are a disparate bunch, sometimes reluctant and cautious. Show us the way, please, Amen.

Persian Lessons

In occupied France in 1942 a young Belgian, Gilles, is arrested with a group of other Jews and taken away to be shot. However, he pleads for his life claiming to be Persian rather than Jewish. (An idea which came from being given a Persian book as they were being transported away.) On hearing this the guards take him to a labour camp where one of the officers is desperate to learn Farsi, the Persian language. A

155

language Gilles does not actually know. So Gilles begins an extraordinary existence, creating a language from scratch and teaching it to officer Klaus Koch. He fears being found out and every day lives on a knife edge.

In the camp Gilles has to record the names of the other inmates, crossing them out when they are taken away to die. When he serves up the food at mealtimes he asks each person for their name. Gilles draws on these names to create words for his version of Farsi. However, when the camp is liberated we discover something else. Gilles remembers these names and can recite every one. Thousands of them. At one point in the film he tells Koch that the prisoners are only anonymous and forgettable to the guards because they don't know their names. At which point I began to think about the biblical promise that our names are etched on the palms of God's hands. (Have a look at Isaiah 49 v 16 and John 10 v 28.) Early in the gospels of Matthew and Luke we find long lists of Jesus's ancestors. In the book of Nehemiah there are lists of all those working on rebuilding the walls of Jerusalem. There are other places in the Good Book where groups of people are recorded. All remembered. Names that mean little to us and yet are known by God.

You only have to Google your own name to discover no one is unique. There are lots of Dave Hopwoods around. And yet, God knows us all. Understands us all. Counts us as precious. We are not merely a number to him, not just another face in the crowd. Not another statistic. Even though a mother forget her child, I cannot forget you, says the Lord. So the prophet Isaiah writes in chapter 49 and verse 15 of his book. We may feel forgotten, disregarded, overlooked by a busy, distracted, ambitious world. But we have a heavenly father, a good kind father, who will never forget us or lose sight of us. May that knowledge give us strength, courage and patience for all that we need to do today.

Parasite

A tale of two families, one rich, one poor. One privileged, the other doing its best to grab a share of that wealth and privilege. It's a riveting, startling tale of cunning forced entry. It begins when Ki Woo, who already has a job with the wealthy Park family teaching their daughter, pretends his sister is a friend who is a qualified art tutor who could teach the Parks' son. Little by little the whole family infiltrate the Parks' privileged existence.

Money dominates so much of life. Activist Shane Claiborne wrote that we are all addicted to it. Which is true really. We can't live without it, not in this kind of world. Interestingly, Jesus didn't condemn money, he understood how much it filled our thinking. On one occasion he told a tale of a shrewd manager, in Luke 16, using money to bless others. The manager had been fired after rumours of misconduct. So he blessed all those who owed his ex-boss money by slashing their bills, and that blessed his ex-boss, as word would travel round that community that the boss was a generous, debt-forgiving man. It's the money that is the star of this twisty tale. And

Jesus winds up by encouraging his hearers to use 'unrighteous mammon' (dosh) to benefit others, and in so doing we will be storing up other kinds of riches – un-rustable, non-stealable, treasures in heaven. An attitude that will also enrich us on earth.

Rebecca

'I dreamt last night I went to Manderley again...'

When an unnamed lady's companion meets rich aristocrat Maxim de Winter in Monte Carlo, it's not long before the two embark on a whirlwind romance and engagement. By the time Maxim returns to Manderley, his large country home, he is married to the second Mrs de Winter. The first of course was Rebecca, and she still casts a long and chilling shadow over the place. In an ill-advised moment, Maxim's new wife appears dressed as Rebecca, thinking he will appreciate the transformation. Instead he is mortified.

The entire de Winter household is gripped by the past. And the new Mrs de Winter finds herself drawn into this captive situation. The spectre of Rebecca is there in everything and it seems that no one can move on. There is a telling moment when the blonde second Mrs de Winter is brushing her hair, only to find dark brown hairs deep within the brush. The past can place its claws within us and steer our futures. It's only when the truth surfaces in Manderley that these people have a chance to break free.

So many of us get snarled up in the past. Perhaps we all do to a greater or lesser degree. We are shaped by our experiences. And not all of that shaping is bad. We learn so much from the good and bad moments. Jesus spoke of the way the truth can set us free. I guess many of us will spend much if not all of our lives working out how to benefit from that promise, what it means for the truth of Jesus to liberate us from that which holds us back, that which makes life difficult. The white noise of anxiety can play in the background of all we are. The graffiti of the past gets etched on our hearts and it can take a series of miracles to wash it off. There will be breakthroughs. I've known them myself. But it can often feel like one step forward one step back. But we do have the good news of a God who understands our struggles, who's been down to the depths and will never give up on us, never leave us or abandon us.

The Equalizer

Robert McCall doesn't sleep well, so he goes to an all-night diner to read his book and drink his tea. Once there he meets Teri, a young woman being controlled and prostituted by brutal gangsters. Robert is a caring guy and cannot stand idly by as he sees Teri being used and mistreated.

So he steps in to rescue her, and suddenly Robert is no longer the gentle guy in the diner, now he's a man fighting for justice and unafraid to do battle with the bad guys, in favour of the oppressed Teri. Kindness drives him to set captives free. In the time of Jesus people were waiting for a man of justice. Someone who would break the chains of oppression. They knew well some writings of the prophet Daniel (recorded in chapter 7 of his book) – 'As my vision continued that night, I saw someone who looked like a son of man coming with the clouds of heaven. He approached the Ancient One and was led into his presence. He was given authority, honour, and royal power over all the nations of the world, so that people of every race and nation and language would obey him. His rule is eternal – it will never end. His kingdom will never be destroyed.'

Depending when you read this, it may not be too long before another Christmas rises over the horizon to meet us. A time when this man of justice appeared, but not as a powerful giant-slayer like Robert, instead a vulnerable child, starting out on a gritty life. When this child grew up he would help a whole bunch of prostitutes not unlike Teri, and lots of others who were suffering hard lives. Jesus rescued plenty of prostitutes and folk who were oppressed and powerless. Not with the kind of weapons that Robert used, but with the power of his compassion and humility. It's hard for us to get our head around who Jesus was, Philippians chapter 2 gives us a glimpse into the extraordinary way he shunned earthly power and ambition... he was humble, we're told, and he walked the path of obedience that led to his death on a barbaric cross. A death he could so easily have avoided, and yet that miraculous sacrifice was too important, too vital for the lost souls of this world. He refused to fight it or to shun it, but instead chose it. For the likes of Teri, for the likes of you, for the likes of even me. A true man of justice.

County Lines

Tyler is a loner, a fourteen-year-old struggling to find his way. He does what he can to care for his little sister but finds himself at odds with his mum and those in authority at school. As a result he is drawn into the dark and sordid world of drug distribution.

He is befriended by Simon, a stranger who seems to care about him. Before long the friendship develops into a business arrangement and Tyler finds himself in a strange and squalid apartment, having transported a packet of drugs to another town. This is a grim and unsettling watch, a story based on real experiences. The writer/director Henry Blake was a youth worker for eleven years. As Tyler spirals downwards his 'friendship' with Simon splinters, and it's not long before he finds himself cast adrift and in very grave danger. This may not be a film you'll ever choose to watch, but just knowing that this story exists in one sense is enough. The chilling statistic appears on screen at the end – 10,000 youngsters are involved in drug distribution in this country. Some as young as eleven.

This frightening and disturbing film portrays a slice of life that leaves us in no doubt that evil is very real in this world. 'Why do the evil prosper?' Jeremiah cries at the start of chapter 12 of his book. 'Why do they thrive?' This is an ancient problem. Sin is not a popular word these days, but whether we call it... misdemeanour, crime, wrongdoing, rebellion, bad... whatever... it strikes me that the long-standing biblical view that this world needs rescuing is a true and sure one. We may develop and advance in many positive ways, yet we are still selfish, self-absorbed people. Just remember the rush for toilet paper, pasta and handwash at the beginning of the pandemic in 2020. It may not be the same as ruining lives with drugs, but we still need rescuing. I do. Every day I am in danger of getting caught in the mud and mire of my own foolish and selfish ways. But the writer of Psalm 139 (verses 7-12) assures us that no place is too dark for God. He is not afraid of the gloom and the grime of real life. Jesus was a realist. Very perceptive. He commented on the kind of things that can come out of us. Gossip. Slander. Evil intentions. Crime. Betrayal. Greed. Envy. I don't think he was focussed on wrongdoing he just didn't pretend, and neither did he cover up. Or say it'll all be all right in the end. Instead he embraced life, all of life, the grim and the gracious. He loved life. And he started something. A way through this mire. He offered us a cross and a crossroads. A decision to make. A light for the gloom.

Official Secrets

Official Secrets is based on the true story of Katharine Gun. Whilst working at GCHQ she saw an email about the U.S. and the U.K.

attempting to coerce other smaller U.N. nations to vote for going to war in Iraq. Torn in two by her loyalty to her job and her sense of justice she wrestled with what to do about this. Eventually she told a friend and anti-war campaigner. Things took on a life of their own and before Katharine knew what was happening the email had been published in the Observer. Everything fell apart, and the life she knew fell away from her.

This is a film which stirs up those questions about fighting for justice and doing the right thing. 'Let justice roll down like a river...' Amos cried out in his book (in chapter 5 verse 24). What I wanted to reflect on now though was the way life often seems beyond our control. Things run away from us, our sense of being in control founders, life becomes too big to handle. I guess many of us have felt that in this pandemic year. We are reminded of our fragility. Which was always there, but before we felt we had a sense of order and regularity about things.

Anything can upend our living. Life is precarious. Which is why, I guess, Jesus encouraged us to build on something solid. Not of our own making, but of God's. In the Bible, time and again, people find things have run away from them. In Jesus's day life was controlled by the Romans, there was an intense desire for freedom, for control, for peace. Which is why, on Palm Sunday, the crowds lined the streets hailing Jesus as the new king, the one who would solve their problems. But Jesus knew that life is always going to be unruly for us, he lived through many troubles himself, and he offered us another way. A daily centring back on him. The solid foundation amidst the storms and uncertainty. The one who can guide, strengthen and comfort us in our trouble and fear. 'Don't bother with religion,' he once said, 'it'll only wear you out. Instead bring your lives to me, and find purpose and strength and rest from your exhausting burdens. Find another way to cope, another way to make it through today.' That's my take on Matthew chapter 11 v 25-30.

Hook

I was reading this week about David fighting Goliath. (In Pete Wilcox's book *Walking the Walk*.) In 1 Samuel 17, David refused to wear the king's armour, which was a massive and risky thing to do. He might offend the king, and leave himself vulnerable. But he knew he had to fight the giant his own way. As himself. Saul and the rest of the army had their own ideas about the best way to battle on, but David was different. He was going to get through as a shepherd boy, not a soldier. If he had marched up to Goliath with a sword and a spear for the usual kind of combat he knew Goliath would floor him in a sneeze. Instead he kept his distance, and remembered how God helped him to fight bears and lions. Goliath made for a big target, the downside of being a giant, and so with a prayer and a well-aimed smooth stone he brought the monolithic monster crashing down.

There's a moment I love in the film *Hook*. Peter Pan has grown up and blended into normal life. He has a family and a high-pressure job. But along the way he has forgotten a few important things. And so he is called back to Neverland, and there he meets The Lost Boys once more. Almost all of them doubt his identity, but just one (sometimes that's all it takes) just one thinks he sees a little more. Is Peter still in there somewhere? Inside the layers piled on by the world. He pulls Peter's face about a bit, takes a closer look, then cries out, 'There you are Peter!'

I find myself constantly battling to be what I think others want me to be, the crucial phrase here being 'what I think others want me to be'. It's probably not the best way to live but it's a battle all the same. It's easy enough to say I should just be myself, but it's not that straightforward. I think I fear upsetting people if I'm too much myself. Which is why I need reminders. Like this tale of David. He didn't fear upsetting the king, he knew he had to be himself. It was the best way. It would help others. I have this birthday card from a few years ago that I keep on a shelf in my office. Another reminder – so I'll leave you with the quote on it: *Why blend when you were born to stand out.* Along with a quote from the Message Bible: 'Because of the cross of Jesus, I have been... set free from the stifling atmosphere of pleasing others and fitting into the little patterns that they dictate.' (Galatians 6 v 14-15)

A Call to Spy

This film tells the true story of the network of spies established early in World War Two in occupied France. 'Spymistress' Vera Atkins is commissioned to enlist courageous and resourceful women for the drop into dangerous territory, with the aim of building a resistance behind enemy lines. Virginia Hall and Noor Inayat Khan, both unlikely spies, risked everything as they undertook their vital roles.

There are lots of examples of covert agents in the Bible. Caleb and Joshua, once part of a twelve-man spy network, drop into enemy territory at the start of the book of Joshua, in order to check out hostile territory. In the unravelling events Rahab takes up the spying mantle when she chooses to hide them from the enemy, and in doing so she goes down in history, her acts of heroism recognised as an expression of faith and dedication (Hebrews 11 v 31). Queen Esther also took on a kind of spying role when her cousin informed her of the secret operation to destroy her own people. Working covertly, prayerfully and courageously she got on with the job of righting that dark wrong, using her skills to change the course of history (Esther 4 v 13-17). In occupied Israel, Mary and Joe would risk their lives smuggling their precious tiny child out of Bethlehem to Egypt, escaping the horrors of Herod; and thirty years later another Mary, with her sister Martha, would regularly offer a covert hideout for Jesus whenever he needed to escape the pressure of the crowds and the danger of arrest. (Matthew 21 v 17 and John 11 & 12)

In a very different way, perhaps there is a sense in which we are all called to be agents in occupied territory from time to time, commissioned to do secret acts that speak of kindness and hope, scuppering the ammunition dumps of cynicism and despair wherever we come across them. It sounds as if I'm exaggerating, but it's not always an easy challenge to stand up and speak up for truth and compassion and faith, when peer pressure would invite us to tread another path; or to remain silent when gossip, criticism and nastiness fill the airwaves. 'It's small things that change the world,' activist Shane Claiborne once said. And we may often wonder whether small things are really worth it. But Jesus urges us that our heavenly father sees all the covert acts we do to challenge any negative status quo. And what about those ongoing faithful 'ordinary' tasks so many perform day in and day out, caring for others, those things which speak of grace and the wonder of the one who left heaven on a mission to serve.

Pride & Prejudice & Zombies

Yes. Really. No kidding.

This is a film that fuses two genres my daughter loves – Jane Austen romances and shock horror scary stories. In this world the Bennett girls are all rather handy with swords and lethal weapons as the black plague has unleashed a tidal wave of the undead. So will Lizzy Bennett and Mr Darcey still manage to get together, whilst doing battle with a myriad of rotting robots?

This macabre tale does still follow the original rather faithfully, with the likes of polite Mr Bingley, smarmy Mr Collins and dastardly Mr

Wickham showing up in fine style to woo the Bennett sisters, and all the while Mother Bennett is gloriously over the top as she attempts to marry off her less-than-genteel, gun-toting clan. Watching this it struck me that you have to really love a story to then do a good job of messing about with it. So although it might seem shocking I'm sure the writers of P&P&Z have a lot of affection for the original.

Jesus was always playing around with Old Testament tales, revising and retelling them in order to grab his listeners and help them understand the new way of life he was offering.

Abraham bantering with God (Genesis 18 v 22-33) became a powerless widow haggling with an unjust judge in Luke 18. Heartless Nabal (1 Samuel 25) refusing to share his wealth with David turned into a rich fool (Luke 12 v 13) who just kept on building bulging barns till the stress killed him. The wise and foolish women from Proverbs 7 & 8 morphed into a couple of smart and silly builders constructing their lives on different foundations (Matthew 7 v 24). And Jesus would revisit the party-throwing wise woman again (in Proverbs 9) when retelling his story of a king inviting people to a sumptuous bash (Luke 14 v 16). Jesus took well known cultural stories and surprised the crowds with them, so they would discuss, question, understand and be drawn towards what he was offering them. Perhaps most famously the runaway boy came limping home in Luke 15, not filthy rich like Jacob in Genesis 33, but just filthy. And lost. And knowing how much he needed his welcoming, kind and generous father.

Jesus didn't just adapt these ancient tales as a gimmick, it was his vital way of communicating the nature of his extraordinary heavenly father.

Back in the late 70s the Riding Lights Theatre Company came up with *The Parable of the Good Punk Rocker*. It was powerful stuff because back then punk was anarchic and fearful. And here were this bunch of Christians turning the punk into a rescuing hero. They took that old Samaritan and gave him ripped clothes and a spiky attitude and haircut. I wonder what stories Jesus might tell today? The parable of the lost car keys? A king sending out party invitations on Twitter and Instagram... to a Zoom meeting for anyone who wanted to discover a new life? Bring your own fatted calf and fine wine. 'This kingdom is like a YouTube clip,' he might say, 'once it is sown online viewers from all over the world come and find hope in its visuals and story.'

First and Last

I finally rediscovered this film this week. I had been trying to track it down for years, an 80s TV movie about a near-60-year-old, desperate to walk from Land's End to John o' Groats. The drama documents Alan's difficulties as he treks from Cornwall to the far reaches of Scotland, falling at many hurdles along the way. Superman he is not. Meanwhile, in the background his family wrestle with their own lives and try to understand why on earth he should want to do this at his time of life.

Alan gives little away. He has a gentle smile which seems to be his stock-in-trade response to most questions and, like many of us men, he doesn't wear his heart on his sleeve. He may just be too private, or he may not have the words to express the deep longings within him. Either way he has to walk, he has to make this journey. Something he has talked about for a long time. His family want it all to be over, and keep planning celebratory parties for his return, a big finish for him. But to Alan the walk is the thing. The travelling. The action of placing one foot in front of the other. Overcoming the odds, proving himself.

The image of life as a journey is beyond overused. We cannot help but keep on describing our lives as times of travelling. There is after all a lot of to-ing and fro-ing. Trips to the shops, ferrying folks about, getting from A to B. All good and vital stuff. But there are different kinds of travelling. Most of my moving about is to keep busy. Helping me achieve things. Alan's walking is about something else. A stepping aside from the rush and the pressure. A letting go.

I have just come across a German proverb which says, 'What is the use of running when we are not on the right road?' I rush about too much I know. Hopefully on some of the right roads. Jesus walked a lot. It was his main form of transport. Those he met had their plans and ideas for how he might spend his time, and sometimes he responded, but at other times he was in no hurry to achieve things. He was never in a rush. He made time for others, and he also made time to be with his father. To step out of life's traffic.

There is a moment in Mark's gospel early one morning, when he is hiding away so he can slow down and be with his father (Mark 1 v 25-38). His friends come bustling, looking for him because lots of folks want his attention. He's becoming famous! He has lots of Facebook friends! He'd better make the most of it. But Jesus's response is clear and simple. He is moving on. There are others who need him and he is not afraid to say no in this situation. Perhaps his time of R&R with his father gave him the insight and the strength to do this. He wasn't after all trying to rush around and achieve lots of things. He was here to be fully human, fully alive. For the sake of the rest of us.

BlacKkKlansman

When new cop Ron Stallworth starts work for the Colorado police department, he decides to call up the Ku Klux Klan and ask to join them. Just one snag. Ron is black, the first black cop in Colorado.

Ron teams up with Flip Zimmerman, himself a Jew, so that Ron can do the phone calls to the KKK while Flip can show up at meetings. Together they will infiltrate the local organisation and see what trouble is brewing. This is a disturbing and shocking movie rife with racism, but doing so to highlight the nature of the problem. It also manages to weave a good deal of humour in the telling of this true tale. Ron's phone calls to the Klan are shot through with irony. Ron will not be pushed down or held back in his bold quest for truth and justice.

When Paul writes about people in a couple of his letters he clearly states his case – all are equal. (Have a glance at Colossians 3 v 11 and Galatians 3 v 28.) There are no divides, no hierarchies, no separation. Men, women, slave, free, black, white, rich, poor, strong, weak, privileged or powerless. All are brought together in Jesus. He breaks down the walls of heartache and hatred, peer pressure and society. He crosses the lines we draw and busts out of the boxes we assemble. Love cannot be conquered by evil and in Jesus we are drawn towards the light of reconciliation, friendship and true humanity. It's a powerful statement of the sacrificial, resurrection love that cannot be conquered by malice or prejudice. The light of Jesus shines in the darkness and the darkness cannot quench it (John 1 v 4-5).

Mickey Blue Eyes

There is a scene in this gangster comedy that I've always loved. Michael's life is going swimmingly, he works in an auction house, and is in love with his fiancée. But then he discovers that his fiancée is the daughter of a mobster. Before long he finds himself going with his mobster prospective father-in-law to meet another couple of goodfellas in a restaurant, and in doing so he needs to pretend he is one of the hoods – 'Micky Blue'. There then follows a series of mishaps as mild-mannered Michael does his level best to appear aggressive and dangerous. To maintain the pretence he even goes so far as practically assaulting his startled, bemused boss from the auction house, hurling him out of the restaurant.

At times I feel as if I've muddled through life adopting various personas to try and fit in. Bank clerk Dave. One of the lads Dave. Sunday morning Dave. Saturday night Dave. Pub Dave. Competent-at-living-this-thing-called-life Dave. Good-at-being-a-Christian Dave. It's one of the snags of being a performer I guess. I have found the work of author and speaker Adrian Plass so refreshing over the years, as he manages to disarm me, to strip back the pretence to what really matters. Adrian and his wife Bridget have been lately posting up podcast reflections, if you'd like to hear one or two just search for Adrian Plass on YouTube.

Years ago as a teenager, I watched a filmstrip (remember them?) called *In the Bin.* I've probably written about it before. It made a deep impression. It's about a man with a cupboard full of masks, one for when he talks to the boss, one for his secretary, a happy one, a grumpy one etc. Then one day a dustbin man turns up, empties his cupboard and takes them all away. The man is horrified! How will he cope without his masks? I have felt like that many times over the years. The dustbin man is Jesus. Unmasking us. Not to leave us vulnerable and ridiculed, but so that we might break through to the real us. The us made in the image of God. With the unique hues and shades that we each possess. It's an ongoing battle to break through the pretence, isn't it? But I'm grateful for the help of a God who won't settle for a contrived version of me with a mask on, even though I frequently go back to that cupboard of fronts and fakery. It's instinctive to want to hide. But the Bin Man understands.

Rush

In the hot summer of 1976 two men kept climbing into cars and chasing each other around a track. One was a party animal, with a hankering for the good life, the other was a single-minded, meticulous technician. Both were intent on winning. However, when Niki Lauda and James Hunt came to race in the German Grand Prix at Nürburgring the weather was not hot and sunny, it was stormy and dangerous and the drivers decide to vote on whether to race that day. Niki was against doing so, but lost the vote. 'It helps if people like you...' James says to Niki after winning the vote. However, as popular as James Hunt was, it was Lauda who saw things more clearly. The race ended in disaster with Niki Lauda hospitalised with terrible injuries.

Popularity is, well... popular these days. We are all encouraged to get more followers, more friends, more 'likes' on social media. To look right so that others will want a piece of us. But Niki Lauda was not interested in that kind of thing. He saw things clearly and wasn't afraid to go against the crowd. One of the things I find difficult about being a Christian is that we are called to walk another road. One that sometimes goes against popular opinion. (Yikes! I like to be liked!) Jesus described it as a narrow way (Matthew 7 v 13-14). A choice that would not necessarily prove a popular or common one. Yet he also described it as the way to life. The poet Robert Frost once wrote of a road less travelled. Which is another way of looking at it. *Two roads diverged in a wood and I, I took the one less travelled by and that has made all the difference.*

Following that road less travelled is not always straightforward, we each of us have to wrestle with the options laid before us, sometimes on a daily basis. And as the writer James puts it in his biblical letter, we need to pray for wisdom so we don't get thrown about in life's storms, torn ragged by the tides of peer pressure and opinion. 'If you don't know what you're doing,' James tells us, 'pray to the Father. He loves to help. You'll get his help, and won't be condescended to when you ask for it. Ask boldly, believingly, without a second thought' (James 1 5-8). It's not always easy to be bold and full of faith in our praying, but just bringing it all to God is a great place to start. To ask for his help, and offer up our struggles and worries to him. 'Don't worry about anything,' writes Paul, 'instead, pray about everything; tell God your needs, and don't forget to thank him for his answers' (Philippians 4 v 6).

A Bridge Too Far/Hacksaw Ridge

There is a shocking scene in *A Bridge Too Far* where Major Cook leads his men across the Waal river in flimsy boats under fire from the enemy on the far shore. They are attempting to take the bridge at Nijmagen under great duress. It's a chilling scene, akin perhaps to the men in the First World War going over the top of the trenches directly into the line of fire.

As they row the Major starts to pray, 'Hail Mary full of grace…' over and over and over. A cry for help as they battle with all their might to reach the far side. I read an old proverb recently, 'Pray to God but row to shore.' Pete Greig quotes it in one of his books. He is talking about prayer and action. The two going hand in hand. Which puts me in mind of another scene, this one from another true war story. *Hacksaw Ridge.* In this scene Desmond Doss, a medic, finds himself witnessing the killing and wounding of all the men in his company. He wonders what to do and cries out to God for help. Then he hears the cry of a wounded soldier and takes that to be God's voice to him.

As Desmond carries man after man to the cliff edge, so he can lower them to safety, he keeps praying, 'One more, help me get one more.' He prays with all he's got and he works with all he's got. This is often the way in life. Prayer and action are not opposites, or contradictory. And our praying doesn't need to be tidy or articulate or use a certain kind of language. Many of my prayers are ragged, and open-ended. Honesty and reality are the best guides. In the book of Esther in the Bible, Esther prays and fasts, and then throws not one but two feasts for the king, so she can find a way to tell him that her people are in grave danger. She uses her wits and courage and wisdom. And she prays. Jesus regularly took time out in the early morning to spend time with his father. Preparing himself for all the work he would do each day. We pray to God, and row for the shore.

The Martian

When a storm hits the planet Mars the group of astronauts exploring the place are forced to head back for their ship so they can escape. However, in the ensuing chaos one man gets injured and left behind. Thinking he is dead the rest of the team head off on their epic journey back to earth. When Mark Watney wakes up he has to think fast and science his way out of a dark problem. He is a long way from home with limited resources on a hostile planet. Somehow he must find a way to survive.

Against the odds Mark starts to grow potatoes on Mars. Using his own... ahem... poo as fertiliser. He is a survivor and a resourceful fighter, so he finds ways to make it through. But for a while no one has any idea that he exists anymore. At one point Mark comments, 'I'm the first person to be alone on their own planet.' And that comment put the thought in my head, yes, but he's not the first person to *feel* alone on their own planet. Mother Theresa is remembered as saying that loneliness is an epidemic of the western world. It's possible to be in a crowded room and feel as if you're the last person on earth.

Back to *The Martian*... at one point on earth Mark tells a group of budding astronauts that they will most certainly face problems. It will happen. They will feel like giving up. At that point what they need to do is solve one problem. Then move on to the next. One snag at a time. One hiccup at a time. Keeping going. Perseverance. One step at a time. Then another. PE coach Joe Wicks, now famous for his workout sessions and healthy eating books, began by offering boot camps in a couple of London parks. He would get up early each morning and wait for folks to pitch up. No one came. No one. But he wouldn't give up. He went to tube stations and handed out flyers, inviting folks to come. Joe says that he had this voice in his head saying, 'Don't give up.'

One of the great themes of the Bible is perseverance. Every single character in the Good Book had to press on. It was not easy for any of them. They had battles, struggles and uphill climbs. But there is a constant voice coming through these tales to us. 'Don't give up.' Fix your eyes on Jesus and keep going. One hiccup at a time. One snag at a time. One step at a time. 'Let's fix our eyes on the one who gave everything for us, the author of life's great story. The one who gave us our faith, our hope and our love. Set your eyes on him, and don't give up' (Hebrews 12 v 1-2).

Wimbledon

Peter Colt is on his last legs. Well, his last tennis legs anyway. He's giving up after one final year at Wimbledon, expecting to bow out in the first round. But it doesn't happen. Incredibly he wins, and then wins again. And yet again. Till he finds himself in the final. He's like a new man, a player inspired. It might just have something to do with him falling for top tennis star Lizzie Bradbury.

There is a moment, on men's finals day, when Peter walks out of his hotel lift to find all of the hotel staff lined up to applaud him and wish him the best for the match. It's a lovely moment, everyone wanting to share in this good time, loaded with hope and possibility. It lifts Peter's spirits. I remember watching this film before Andy Murray had ever won Wimbledon, it all seemed a bit of a dream come true, even if it was just on the big screen. I grew up watching Bjorn Borg win year after year. Wimbledon was the only tournament we ever saw so I never saw him lose, no matter how hard the matches were, till 1981. He lost in the final that year to one John McEnroe – and I was devastated, I just didn't think it was possible.

'If you can meet with Triumph and Disaster and treat those two impostors just the same...' These lines from Kipling's poem are quoted on Wimbledon's centre court. A reminder that neither of these is enough to satisfy our deep human longings.

We can't all win all the time. In fact life is fraught with failure and difficulties. But it's great to share sometimes in the good news of others. It feels as if we have another chance too. Thinking about it now, in a strange kind of way, Peter Colt coming out of that lift reminds me of a carpenter from Nazareth riding into town (on a colt, no less!) and folks turning out in their droves to see him. Lining up to applaud and cheer and wish him the best on his journey to change things. Folks had hoped then for a triumphant display of power and skill. What they got looked all wrong. Jesus lost. Ended up looking like the failure. No final big serve to win the match. But in his losing he sided with all the rest of us when our lives get upended. When we fall off the track once more. When we sit heartbroken and disappointed. Jesus losing on that cross ushered in another age. An age of profound help for all of us, for a universe in pain. Not a quick fix or cheap solution, but a way to know the presence and friendship of God in every moment of loss and gain, every cheer, sob, smile and call for help. He is on our side.

Unbroken – Path to Redemption

A sequel to Angelina Jolie's movie *Unbroken*, this is the true story, based on Laura Hillenbrand's powerful biography, of the post-war struggles of a very damaged man, and his quest to find hope.

When Olympic athlete Louis Zamperini returned from World War Two, having suffered terribly in a prisoner of war camp in Tokyo, he was a man secretly in bad shape. Haunted by his experiences he struggled to sleep and fight off the flashbacks. Little by little drink took a hold, until his brother sought him out in a bar. 'You're not man enough to get help,' Pete told him honestly when Louis refused to go with him. Pete knew his younger brother well, he had rescued him from a life of teenage crime when he first taught him to run. Before the war Louis came close to breaking the four-minute mile, just seven seconds off. But the war and injury brought an end to his medal winning hopes.

Hurting so much, haunted terribly by what he's lived through, Louis is a man at war with himself, at war with a sense of failure and loss.

We men do not find it easy to admit weakness, to talk of nightmares, pains and fears. We feel we should be all right. Be able to cope. Be tough. But sometimes the best thing we can do is to let go of our weakened and wounded strength, to draw on the strength of another. That's the thing about Jesus, he is not merely a good example to follow, he holds within himself the ability to help us to follow. However falteringly we may travel. Not because we're strong enough, but because he is, not merely self-help, but his help. So much so that a man like Louis, having suffered the worst kind of merciless savagery, could find a new way forward, a new life, fresh forgiveness for his wounded history. Peace for the war he was still fighting within himself. The conflict finally over.

I find myself regularly wrestling with what I think I should do to appear blokey, sorted or cool. But life is found elsewhere, I'm sure of it. In true humanity. Jesus lived it and offers a hand to help us lean towards his way. In our weakness God comes through, so the activist formerly known as Saul wrote to us in the Good Book. And he went further, not being afraid to talk of his weaknesses so God could shine through. That's a big ask – to offer God our weaknesses. And extraordinarily difficult in a world of glamorous images of strength and kudos. But

Jesus spoke of God knowing us truly, seeing all that we do and all that we aspire to and long to be. The secret longings to be different. God understands and keeps nudging us towards his vulnerable heart. And another way.

The Mission

Mendoza is a slave trader racked with guilt about killing his brother in a duel. As a form of penance he elects to climb a huge waterfall, dragging his armour, the tools of his murderous trade, behind him. He struggles and falls in places, the climb is so steep, but he refuses to give in., When he eventually makes it to the top he is confronted by a man with a knife, a member of the tribe he has been enslaving. They stare at each other for a moment. Then the man moves towards him, flashes the knife... and cuts him free of his burden, hurling it into the water below. Those that Mendoza was enslaving are the ones able to cut him free.

I've often thought that scenes from movies, like any art form, can mean all kinds of things to us, depending on when we see them. And this scene of lugging a huge burden up a catastrophic hill is no exception. How often does life feel like this, as if we are battling against the odds, as if things are weighing us down, pulling us back, causing us to flounder. And there are days when we experience a cutting free. A liberation. But there are other days when we wrestle with the burdens again. I used to think that being a Christian was about getting all our problems solved. About reaching a pinnacle of happiness and plain sailing. But life isn't like that. And if today you feel a little like Mendoza, struggling to climb that hill, you are not alone.

So many battle through life. Perhaps we all do. We all know the languages of failure and weakness and uphill struggles. And it's worth keeping in mind that when Jesus stepped onto this planet he didn't come with the intention of avoiding the problems and holding back, instead he threw himself into those climbs and struggles, not afraid of the jagged rocks and torn fingernails, so that he could help us, inspire us, give us extra strength and courage when we need it.

The Beach

Looking for a summer watch recently we settled on revisiting *The Beach*, a film I've loved for a while (the book too). Richard goes looking for paradise, for a new kind of life, something more beautiful, more exciting... and yes, something more dangerous. It's not long before he hears about a secret beach on an island off the coast of Thailand, and hooking up with Françoise and Étienne, he heads off to find this idyllic place, and the community who live there.

I have often thought of this as a Prodigal tale, someone leaving home and going hunting for a better life. I thought initially that it would be about Richard and his mates living a debauched existence on booze and drugs. But that is not really the case. They find a peaceful community with an organised way of life and a work ethic.

Appreciating the privacy and beauty they have found there. However, when two of the 'family' get attacked by a shark the rest don't deal well with them, refusing to take them back to the mainland for treatment. It seems as if all is well as long as all is well. When weakness disrupts the idyll it is not really tolerated. Other problems creep in and before long their community life starts to crumble.

It put me in mind of the true tale of the six boys stranded on a rocky island just off the coast of Tonga in 1966. These young men quickly developed a way of life which included keeping the fire going, a proper work ethic, and dealing with conflict in a healthy way. They began and ended each day with song and prayer, having built their own guitar from driftwood, a coconut shell and steel wires from their wrecked boat. You can read about it here:

www.theguardian.com/books/2020/may/09/t he-real-lord-of-the-flies-what-happened-when-six-boys-were-shipwrecked-for-15-months

In *The Beach* Richard embodies the hunger for more, for a better life. For adventure, colour and a deeper reality. Breaking out of the dull. Something perhaps that many of us relate to from time to time. I think that's a sign of the God-given longing we all have, a divinely inspired restlessness. This present reality is not perfect (even on an idyllic beach) and we have a sense that we were made for more. For a better kind of good. That's what the prodigal is looking for in Luke 15, and when he finds it he discovers it in an unexpected place. To quote T.S. Eliot – 'the end of all our exploring will be to arrive where we started and know the place for the first time.' In a sense we prodigals come home again each day, finding help, home and a welcome in the embrace of a generous father who loves us radically and passionately. Smiling from his heart, and hurling himself towards us with his arms wide open, as he catches the first glimpse of us limping home again.

Babette's Feast

When Babette serves up a sumptuous feast she rocks her small Danish community to the core. When your normal fare is bland, grey gruel... then turtle soup, quails and fine wines are like a tidal wave on the taste buds. Set in the nineteenth century, this is a fabulous story of celebration and grace. Babette wants to bless her strict village. She works as a servant to the late pastor's daughters who live frugally, charitably and carefully. Everyone is poor and life is very serious. Then Babette comes into some money. So she makes plans, and invites all the village around to eat together. Little by little, as the food and wine are shared, colour comes into their lives.

Phillip Yancey dedicated a whole chapter of his book *What's So Amazing About Grace* to this film. It's a great enactment of kindness towards a people who have not done anything to earn it. And it's sumptuous kindness too, it's colourful and lifegiving. It breaks down the walls of loss and pain and heartache. When Jesus wanted to leave us with something that would profoundly remind us of his presence and his redemptive power, what did he choose? A bumper sticker? A t-shirt? An emoji? A tattoo? No. Food. He took a feast which celebrated freedom from slavery and asked us to remember him with it. Food and drink. Bread and wine. The basics of life. Tea and biscuits. Coke and crisps. Burgundy and beef wellington. Food sustains us. It nourishes us. Jesus told his disciples in John 4 v 32 that he had food they didn't know about, a different kind of sustenance that came from connection with his father, and when Jesus spoke to a group of believers in Revelation 3 verse 20 his offer was simple. 'Let us eat together.' It was a deeply symbolic and meaningful invitation. Our lives shared with God's life though his son. Jesus fed thousands of hungry people with bread and fuelled a celebration with the best wedding wine. Bread and wine. A basic reminder. We need food, we need drink, we need Jesus.

The Dark Knight Rises

For all its bangs and crashes, and there are plenty of those in this Batman epic, the most telling and chilling scene occurs after the criminals have taken over the city of Gotham. Innocent folk are dragged to an oddly decorative chair, before a corrupt and merciless judge, in a court devoid of justice. The only verdict each time is death or exile. And exile means death. If ever there was a need for the dark knight to rise, this is the time. Truth and mercy have been flipped on their head. Chaos reigns. We need sense and compassion back in the driving seat. It reminded me of those countries where oppression is the order of the day. Where the innocent are trampled and the weak pushed aside. In too many places corruption and self-interest fog the corridors of power, and even good leaders can get overwhelmed by events or lost in a maze of wrong turns. In his book *Men Behaving Badly*, author John Goldingay suggests that humans were never designed to lead a whole nation or country. The job is just too big. Which is why any leader will fall short, and be an easy target for criticism. We don't have the ability or resources. A task so big is beyond us. We might as well ask a person to flap their arms and fly. We're just not designed to do that job. The prophet Daniel saw a leader who *is* equipped to guide nations. A son of man. A person with the calibre to lead with truth and justice, honour, peace, faithfulness and compassion. Goldingay suggests that leadership is ultimately God's role. And Jesus demonstrated that it begins, not with wielding power, but washing feet. Cherishing people. Listening to them and responding to their crucial needs. Let's pray for our leaders, and for those who who feel disregarded, overpowered, damaged even, by those of us who are more powerful.

In Bruges

This is one of those movies that reminds me a film does not have to be PG rated and squeaky clean to communicate something really powerful about compassion and sacrifice. (It's 18 rated, no more clues.) Ken and Ray are a couple of hitmen hiding out in Bruges for a while. Ken is eternally upbeat, enjoying the sights, art and architecture. But Ray is not happy. He is falling apart and bored by Bruges. Little by little he unravels and Ken finds that he has to be the one to keep things on track. Ray annoys the pants off him but Ken believes in him, wants the best for him, and is willing to lay everything on the line to help him. They make a couple of unlikely friends.

Stickability is tough at times. We live in days when everything seems temporary. Gadgets come with built-in obsolescence, our homes fill with laptops, phones and clothes as we replace them with new stuff. I do anyway. A lot of us do I'm sure. The notion that something is reliable and lasting is strange these days. But Ken is a rock for Ray. While others are out to use and trick them, Ken stays strong. Many of us lack a big story these days, an epic reason for life, the universe and everything. The great news from the Bible is that there is a big story. We are part of an epic. Something that is not temporary or needs replacing in six months. We have a Creator who is a rock we can lean on. A ground zero foundation for us to build on. Our lives have meaning, and though the trends and signs around us might question that, we can find ourselves in the Good Book. And find one who knows the flimsy nature of this life, and is bigger. We have significance. We are not just a speck in the mind's eye of history. We are designed and precious.

Guardians of the Galaxy

The other night I caught the start of the Marvel film *Guardians of the Galaxy*, my wife and older daughter were watching it. I'm less of a superhero fan but I do love the way this irreverent intergalactic tale begins. First up you hear the strains of that unique '70s 10cc classic *I'm Not in Love*, then Chris Pratt boots and shuffles his way through other-worldly puddles and predators in a scene reminiscent of something out of Indiana Jones, all to the Redbone song, *Come and Get Your Love.* It's a great feelgood scene. Even for an old superhero grinch like me. Han Solo was a similarly irreverent, swashbuckling space rebel, and for me the best thing about *Star Wars.* The word irreverent is overused these days, I guess it's come to mean something that bites back against the norm. Marvel heroes aren't perhaps supposed to behave this way. And we may not expect those in the Good Book to either, yet the Bible's full of irreverent heroes. Prophets like Micah, Jeremiah and Ezekiel were forever breaking the rules. Booting and shuffling their way through the expected religious and social norms of their day. And for no small reason. They had glimpsed something of life's reality and knew that behaving 'properly' was not enough. They had to rattle cages and un-float some boats to make people sit up and take notice. Jeremiah buried his pants. Seriously. Stuck 'em in the ground so they'd come up stinking of donkey dung, no doubt he then put them on, over his tights like Superman, to provoke the question – 'Why are you looking an idiot?' 'Because,' rebel

Jerry might reply, 'your focus, your priorities are pants! They're riddled with corruption and without God's help they will fill apart.' On another occasion he likened the people to camels on heat, forever chasing after the next thrill. In an age when I find myself flitting from one online distraction to another, it's still a timely message. For me if no one else. Thank God for that supremely divine rebel, Jesus, who upset so many of the norms, not for the sake of it, but because he knew we needed an open door to another life and a daily fresh start.

The Last Crusade

Indiana Jones and his dad are out there searching for the Holy Grail, the cup used at the last supper. On reaching the caves where this is hidden Indy discovers that he must pass three tests to get to the cup and save his father.

(1) Humility, (2) respecting the name of God and (3) a step of faith. Three vital things in life. For Indy they are crucial tests, we might call them crucial priorities. Following Jesus has always been a unique mixture of hope and challenge. Humility and respect. Comfort and discovery. Steps of reassurance and steps into the unknown.

'Step out of the traffic, take a good long look at me, discover the unforced rhythms of grace. Take up my approach and my ways of living, for they are good. My burdens are light.'

Fantastic, life-giving words of assurance from Jesus in Matthew 11 v 28-30.

But in Matthew 16 v 24-25 he also says, 'Take up your cross and follow me. Lose your life and you will find it.'

Both and. One with the other.

Hope and challenge. Compassion and justice. Truth and love. There is a lovely verse in Psalm 85 which sums this up. 'Wisdom and mercy have embraced. Unfailing love and truth have met together. Righteousness and peace have kissed!'

Jesus brings together these aspects of full life. 'Truth springs up from the earth, and righteousness smiles down from heaven.' Psalm 85 goes on. A cross rises from the dust, fulfilling the promise of new life, on earth as in heaven. And as the sun rises on a resurrection dawn, the Good Father smiles on us from heaven.

Indy is on his way to finding life and healing for his father, but it involves stepping across a valley. Keeping going though the way is uncertain. Though he is afraid and learning as he goes. We face these valleys and need help to keep going. We need wisdom and mercy, love and truth to help us. Winston Churchill famously said, 'When you're going through hell... keep going.' Lord, please help us, today, tomorrow, and the day after that. One step at a time. Amen.

A Fistful of Favourite Films

In no particular order. Apologies if any should send your head spinning in a *I don't believe it* sort of way. There's no accounting for taste.

Raiders of the Lost Ark
Last Action Hero
Terminator 2
Rear Window
Went the Day Well
The Help
The War Wagon
Last of the Mohicans (1992)
The Good the Bad and the Ugly
Sleepers
Grease
West Side Story
Danny the Champion of the World
The Cross and the Switchblade
Blue Like Jazz
633 Squadron
Bridge Over the River Kwai
Gone Girl
Seven
What We Did on Our Holiday
Calvary
In Bruges
LA Confidential
A Shot in the Dark
Notting Hill
Love Actually
The Boat That Rocked

Mamma Mia: Here we go again
Zodiac
The Departed
The Great Gatsby (2013)
Goodfellas
The Commitments
Shallow Grave
Groundhog Day
The Prestige
Bruce Almighty
Evan Almighty
Liar Liar
Patch Adams
The Big Short
Spotlight
Crash (2004)
The Money Pit
Peter's Friends
Pacific Heights
Jaws
Jurassic Park
Jurassic World
Bohemian Rhapsody
Ferris Bueller's Day Off
Memphis Belle
The Killing Fields
Suspicion
Blinded by the Light
Goldeneye
Schindler's List
Hidden Figures
Us
The Sting
Enemy of the State

Mission Impossible: Fallout
The Family Man
The Family Stone
Uncle Buck
Home Alone
JFK
Flushed Away
The Day of the Jackal
Regarding Henry
The Deer Hunter
The Fugitive
Star Wars 7: The Force Awakens
Charade
Where Eagles Dare
Gladiator
Goodbye Christopher Robin
Thelma and Louise
Back to the Future
Cinema Paradiso
The Social Network
Once Upon a Time in Hollywood
Clockwise
Monty Python and the Holy Grail
Captain Underpants
The Family
La La Land
Dead Poets
Sing Street
Pulp Fiction
Shrek
Jojo Rabbit
Papillon (1973)
Yesterday
The Great Escape

The Dam Busters
A Bridge Too Far
The Untouchables
Whistle Down the Wind
Last Temptation
Jesus of Montreal
About a Boy
Brooklyn
Little Women (1994)
Shawshank Redemption
Empire of the Sun
To End All Wars
The Sting
The Cat in the Hat (2003)
I was Monty's Double
Colditz
Ice Cold in Alex
Gone in 60 Seconds
Leon
The Truman Show
The Transporter
Breakdown
Layer Cake
Inception
Passengers
Murder on the Orient Express (1974)
Dan in Real Life
Whiplash
The Highwaymen
The Virtuoso
Escape from Pretoria
Parasite
Eye in the Sky
Official Secrets

That Thing You Do
Millions
Walk the Line
50 First Dates
Hotel Rwanda
Shooting Dogs
Withnail and I
Misery
First and Last
Three Billboards Outside Ebbing, Missouri
While You Were Sleeping
Nativity!
Rush
Chariots of Fire
The Railway Children
Gone Baby Gone
The Bounty
West Side Story (1961)
Con Air
Face/Off (one of the few films with / in the title)
Le Mans 66
The Company Men
The King of Comedy
Jurassic World

'Aloha, auf wiedersehen, bonsoir, sayonara, and all those goodbye things, baby.'

And finally what you might call a post credits moment...

Blessed

Blessed are you when you can muster a smile,
You never know who might get the benefit.
Blessed are you when you pick yourself up
After another stumble or slip.
Blessed are you when you bring peace
Into the life of another.
Blessed are you when you bless someone else,
With your actions and your messages.

Blessed are those who encourage you on today,
Those who are in the right place at the right time.
Blessed are the carers, the helpers, the enablers,
The servants, those doing the everyday tasks.
Blessed are those who comfort others,
And those who help us when the going is hard.
Blessed are the listeners, those who can pause,
Those willing to take time out to hear us and others.

May you find a moment of blessing today,
A moment of good cheer
When you feel your spirits lifted,
A moment when you feel valued
And know how precious you are,
And if that encouragement is not easy to find,
Then may these few words be that moment for you.

Printed in Great Britain
by Amazon